The Metaphysical Cosmos

Cosmic Structure

and

Soul Travel

By Elizabeth M. Hazel

The Metaphysical Cosmos: Cosmic Structure and Soul Travel
Text and illustrations by Elizabeth Hazel © 2025
All rights reserved.

ISBN: 978-1-7353770-2-5

Please do not reproduce text or images without author's
permission; this includes copying and posting images
or text on the internet.

No part of this book may be used as data for 'training' any large language model or as part of any machine learning or neural network architecture.

"Fair Use" laws apply to reviewers, who may quote
short sections of text in reviews (3 to 4 sentences)
and use the book cover image if needed for review purposes.

For permissions, please contact: ehazel1731@gmail.com

Contents

A Brief Introduction..pg i

Part I: The Cosmos and Soul Travel

Chapter 1. Time and Ancient Wisdom..............................pg 1

Chapter 2. The Egyptian Cosmos......................................pg 7

Chapter 3. The Mesopotamian Cosmos............................pg 13

Chapter 4. Changes in Cosmic Time.................................pg 20

Chapter 5. Metaphysical Mythology.................................pg 37

Chapter 6. The Greek Cosmos..pg 53

Chapter 7. Mystery Cults and Soul Travel........................pg 73

Part II: Applied Astrology—Planets, Stars and Souls

Chapter 8. Soul Portals..pg 83

Chapter 9. The Moon's Nodes and Mercury....................pg 97

Chapter 10. Draconic Charts and Other Portals............pg 113

Chapter 11: Applied Astrology: Sample charts

    Syd Barrett..pg 121

    Dane Rudhyar...pg 128

    Audie Murphy..pg 131

    Amalie "Emmy" Noether..pg 140

    Ursula Le Guin...pg 145

Sample Draconic Charts

    Secretariat..pg 150

    Alfred Hitchcock..pg 154

Conclusion..pg 161

References..pg 163

Had we but World enough, and Time,
This coyness Lady were no crime.
We would sit down, and think which way
To walk, and pass our long Loves Day.

...But at my back I alwaies hear
Time's winged Charriot hurrying near:
And yonder all before us lye
Desarts of vast Eternity.

...And while thy willing Soul transpires
At every pore with instant Fires,
Now let us sport us while we may;
And now, like am'rous birds of prey,
Rather at once our Time devour,
Than languish in his slow-chapt pow'r.
Let us roll all our Strength, and all
Our sweetness, up into one Ball:
And tear our Pleasures with rough strife,
Thorough the Iron gates of Life.
Thus, though we cannot make our Sun
Stand still, yet we will make him run.

To His Coy Mistress by Andrew Marvell, English metaphysical poet, born March 31, 1621 in Winestead-in-Holderness, East Riding of Yorkshire, England, and died August 16, 1678.

A Brief Introduction

Welcome, readers! The landmark book **Hamlet's Mill: An Essay Investigating the Origins of Human Knowledge and Its Transmission Through Myth** (1969)[1]* by Georgio de Santillana and Hertha von Dechend was a catalyst for many years of research into the mysterious topic of reincarnation. The authors jump from topic to topic in a series of scholarly essays. Some readers find the book daunting or impenetrable. Useful concepts have to be teased to the surface through multiple re-readings.

The authors of **Hamlet's Mill** makes one thing emphatically clear: *the structure of the cosmos and soul travel are inseparable.*

The Metaphysical Cosmos is based on a lecture given at the SOTA (State of the Art Conference) on October 25, 2014 in Niagara Falls, New York. A great deal of material was cobbled down to fit into a two-hour presentation. People asked if it was available in book form. Now it is. This text includes my original illustrations, Creative Commons and public domain images. Material omitted from the lecture because of time constraints is included in this text.

My primary intent is to provide a comprehensive, not exhaustive, overview of complex entwined concepts. This multi-disciplinary material amalgamates centuries of lore about time, myths, the cosmos, souls, and transmigration transmitted over many centuries, followed by a section dedicated to astrological applications. I'm grateful to my late friend James Holden, Robert Hand, Donna van Toen, and other helpful people who recommended books and nudged me to continue my pursuit of the topic through many phases of research over several years.

New information discovered after 2015 has been collated into the book. There will never be a good stopping point for research. It's entirely possible that a week after this book is released I'll stumble onto another fabulous reference work and much wailing and moaning will ensue. A new stack of books will grow, because in my house books are like bloody Tribbles breeding exponentially under cover of night. Tarot decks do the same thing.

Georgio de Santillana and Hertha von Dechend did a deep dive into ancient cosmic structures and myths in **Hamlet's Mill**. Astrologers are in the best position

---

* To suit my own preference, book citations are in the References section on page 163. Footnotes marked with an asterisk (*) are at the bottom of the page for ease of reading.

to utilize the information in practical ways. Hopefully this text will make the substance of **Hamlet's Mill** more accessible and *au current*, as their material has been supplemented with current scholarship on ancient astrology and archeo-astrology.

Part I is organized into chapters that circle around the main theme of the book—how souls were created and travel through the cosmos. The pieces and parts are reassembled in Part II with a presentation of astrological tools and applications.

Theories about souls, soul travel and fate swirled around the early development of astrology. Those ideas have been lost or garbled over the intervening centuries. Reclaiming those theories makes it clear that birth charts are a singularly useful method for mapping the soul's purpose. My hope is that this book will help astrologers become better equipped to approach charts with the tools necessary to dig into questions about soul purpose for themselves and their clients. A greater understanding of fate and fortune is crucial to helping people reach toward the future to create a better destiny.

April 6, 2025
Toledo, Ohio

Part I

The Cosmos
And
Soul Travel

Chapter 1
Time and Ancient Wisdom

Who are we and why are we here? What's the meaning of life? How did life begin? Who made the earth and the stars? What is the meaning and purpose of the cosmos? And how do human souls travel through the cosmos?

These were questions asked by the metaphysical philosophers of antiquity. People have an enduring interest in finding the answers to these questions.

Aristotle states in Book VI of **Nichomachian Ethics**[1] that the highest virtue is *Theoretical Wisdom*. As I present this material, I don't expect you to believe in it. This is not an attempt at religious conversion. My intention is to share what ancient people believed about the cosmos and soul travel. The bonus is that astrologers are in a good position to understand and make use of this information.

Let's dig into the metaphysical feast.

Ideas About Time
Astrology is the study of time and planetary cycles. There are various ways to think about time.

Human time relates to the lifespan of a long-lived person, perhaps eighty to one hundred years. Planetary cycles that occur in human spans include the Metonic soli-lunar cycles, Mars and Venus cycles, Jupiter-Saturn mutations that occur in twenty-year intervals, and a complete eighty-four year Uranus cycle.

Collective time involves 100+ year spans associated with the duration of societies, dynasties, nations and cultures. These can be examined with outer planet transits and conjunctions. The Jupiter-Saturn conjunctions in one element (180-200 years), Uranus-Neptune and Uranus-Pluto conjunctions. Neptune-Pluto conjunctions occur in roughly 495-year intervals.

Cosmic time is connected with long time periods called aeons or ages. Thinkers in ancient cultures invented many methods of measuring these: the Vedic Yugas, the Mayan Long Count, Egyptian Sothic Cycles, the Arabic Great Years, and the Greek Platonic Years. These huge chunks of time are associated with the rise and fall of mighty civilizations and gods.

Galactic time is the journey of the solar system around the edges of the Milky Way's Galactic Center. It takes 200 million years for our solar system to complete one revolution. The solar system has made approximately twenty to twenty-five revolutions in five billion years of existence. Galactic time is incomprehensible and well outside of the scope of human operations.

Linear and Non-Linear Time

There's also an issue of how time is perceived. People tend to see time as linear, one thing happening after the other in a chronological manner. Non-linear time is composed of event vectors that twirl in spirals and continually intersect in time-space. Imagine looking into a bucket of snakes. The snakes are entwined and overlapping, and in constant motion. It isn't orderly and sequential like linear time. Metaphysical ideas about spiraling time have been restated in quantum physics and ideas like string theory. Ancient thinkers understood non-linear time and had names and symbols for it.

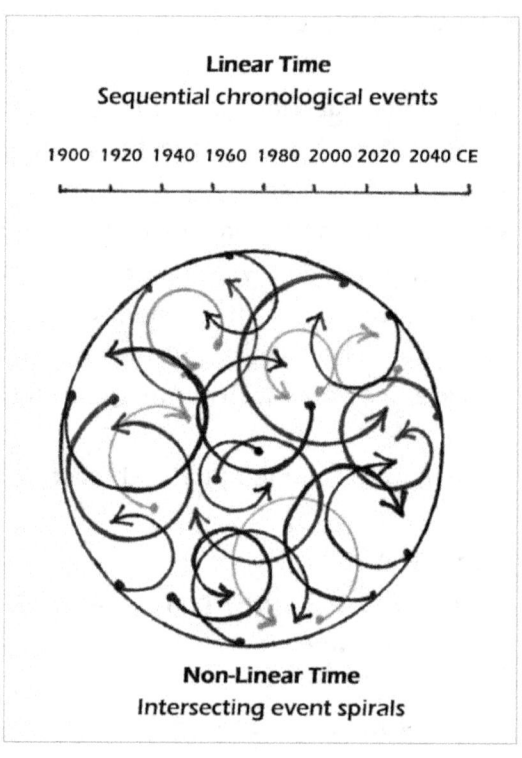

Sources of Ancient Wisdom

How did pre-historic people generate ideas about the cosmos? They relied on a variety of sources.

Ordinary perception: what could be seen with the eyes. Ancient sky-watchers were very good observers who tracked the slow movements of the stars, planets and Sun. Bone and ivory artifacts from around 30,000 BCE are marked with primitive lunar calendars. The cave paintings of bulls and animals in the Salon des Taurees in Lescaux, France, include star maps.

Stone Markers and Constructed Sites: pre-historic sites were constructed to perform various astronomical tasks. Nabta Playa, in the southwest desert of Egypt, features a strange arrangement of rough stone markers. Carbon dating places activity at this site from 11,000 to 6,000 BCE. The current theory is that the stones marked the movement of stars. Star positions were marked over a five-thousand year period, until the area became too dry to inhabit. Nabta Playa is thought to be the oldest site marking astronomical observations on Earth.

Some ancient sites are oriented to the solstice and equinox points. Other sites include stones or construction features that mark star risings and settings. One of the oldest solar observatories is Gosseck Henge in Saxony-Anhalt, Germany, which was built around 5,000 BCE. Avebury Henge is another site that will be discussed more in this book. Early sky-watchers were well aware of the cardinal points of the Sun's apparent annual journey. The stone monolith structures and circles scattered around England and Europe are probably the most familiar, but there are pre-historic sky observation sites all around the globe.

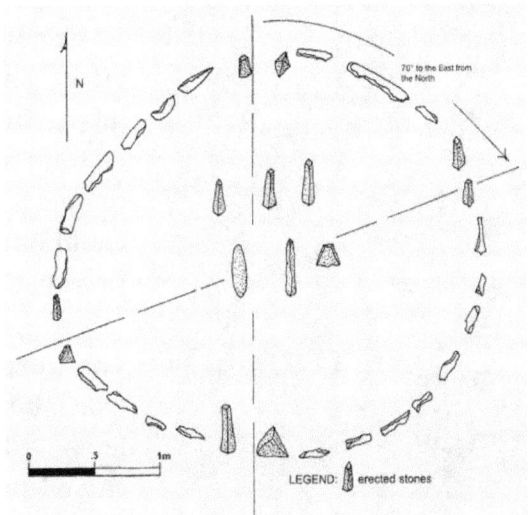

Nabta Playa photo and drawing of the arrangement of stones (Wiki Commons)

Ideas Handed Down Through Generations: keeping track of complex sky movements doesn't require a system of letters and numbers. Before writing was available, wisdom was handed down through oral traditions, stories, and myths. The stone markers and constructed sites mentioned above required a great deal of collective effort over time, as well as exacting designs. Unless you believe these were provided by aliens, giants or fairies, the plans for these sites were designed by humans without writing systems or complex mathematics.

Visionary and Shamanic Exploration: although contemporary culture shuns information obtained through visionary dreams, drug-induced states, or shamanic journeys, this wasn't true of ancient cultures. Non-linear methods of information gathering were perfectly relevant and accepted modes of gaining knowledge about the Earth and the cosmos.

Details on Pillar 43 in Enclosure D.
Credit: German Archeological Institute, photo by Oliver Dietrich, 2009, on the Gobekli Tepi Research Project site.

Gobekli Tepi (Belly Hill) was first noted in 1963, but it wasn't until 1994 that German archeologist Klaus Schmidt recognized its significance and began excavations. The site is in southern Turkey near the border of Syria. It features large pillars carved with bizarre animals and mysterious symbols. Gobekli Tepi was a religious site constructed around 11,000 BCE to 9,500 BCE). The carvings may include astronomical observations but that is, as yet, uncertain. Whatever its purpose, the site was deliberately buried around 8,000 BCE. Much effort went into creating the site, and an equally great effort went into burying it under thousands of tons of soil. It is one of the oldest man-made temple sites found by archeologists *so far*. There could be older, or equally old sites hiding in locations yet to be discovered.

The purpose of Gobekli Tepi was certainly religious, but any thoughts about it are purely speculative. What is very clear just by looking is that the carved pillars depict weird and otherworldly images and symbols that were significant and meaningful to the people who did the carvings. People don't put years of effort into hauling and carving huge rocks weighing five to ten tons for something that's meaningless. It had meaning for them.

Some the animals re recognizable, while others are distorted. The use of hallucinogenic substances in shamanic or religious ceremonies is persistent throughout world history. Maybe the designers of Gobekli Tepi were ingesting *Amanita muscaria* (psilocybin mushrooms). It will be some time before the site is fully excavated and even then it may not reveal all of its secrets.

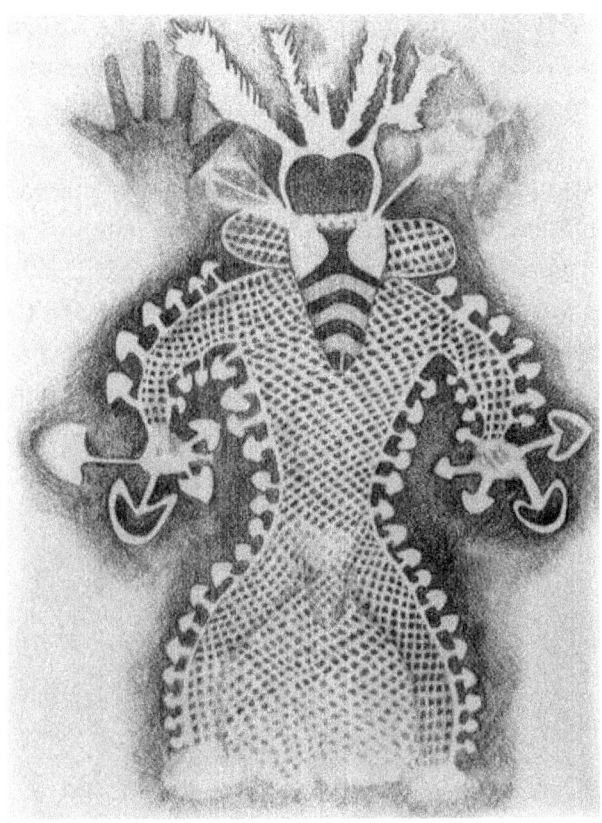

Bee-faced mushroom shaman of Tassili n'Ajjer, Algeria, 9,000-6,000 BCE. Drawing of petroglyph by Kat Harrison in *Psilocybin: The Magic Mushroom Grower's Guide,* 1986 pg 71.
Used with the artist's kind permission.

Ancient peoples were excellent observers of their environment and of the sky. They built large structures and placed stones to record of celestial movements. Knowledge and wisdom were passed through multiple generations. At least some of that knowledge was acquired through visionary exploration. Little by little, archeologists are finding evidence of detailed celestial knowledge that extends back to 15,000 BCE and earlier.

The earliest literate civilizations that have had the most influence on Western thought—the Egyptians and Mesopotamians—didn't emerge from nowhere, and they didn't suddenly acquire oodles knowledge about celestial movements. We tend to think of these civilizations as the earliest human cultures. They were not. They were simply more organized, had writing and numeric systems, and left constructed sites that still remain. Knowledge about Sun, Moon, planet and star cycles was probably passed down from much earlier peoples. There's evidence that humans were aware of lunar cycles from 30,000 BCE, and information tends to accumulate. It's told to someone who passes the information to another person. This process rolled along quite efficiently until people invented writing systems were able to write things down to share with others.

A great deal of celestial knowledge existed before anyone was able to write it down. Humans have existed in their current form, Homo sapiens, for around 80,000 to 100,000 years. Did humans suddenly get smart just because somebody figured out how to write? Doubtful. The human brain hasn't changed much in all that time. People who rely on their environment for survival have to be good observers. The sky is as much a part of the environment as the landscape. Writing and record-keeping are, in human terms, relatively new. Oral transmission and mnemonic skills served humanity for tens of thousands of years before writing was developed.

Chapter 2

The Egyptian Cosmos

The missing links between Egyptian star lore and Hellenic astrology are being found. Books and articles detailing new discoveries have been published in recent years. The new material contradicts ideas about the Egyptians that have been promulgated by Egyptologists since that field got started in the early 1800s, after Napoleon and his troops looted sites and brought artifacts back to France. The Rosetta Stone, discovered in the 1830s, helped efforts to translate Egyptian hieroglyphs, but it wasn't a perfectly comprehensive translation key. A lot of early mistakes have been passed down through generations of Egyptologists. There are a vanguard of people producing new translations.

The Egyptians were obsessed with time and the soul's journey into the afterlife. They were astute star-watchers and fantastic record-keepers. They were also good at keeping their wisdom a secret and preventing transmission to other cultures. The Egyptians didn't like foreigners, their beliefs or influences. They believed their ways were superior, more ancient, and more sacred.

Egyptian religion and cosmology were a sophisticated distillation of time-keeping based on the movements of the Sun, stars, and planets. The sky was the clock that marked the proper times for annual and seasonal rituals, processions, re-enactments, and agricultural activities.

Egyptian funerary art and scrolls feature lists of decans. Greek and Roman writers never mentioned Egyptian constellations, but they did mention the decans or faces. It's becoming apparent that the Egyptians didn't use constellations. They started trading with the Mesopotamian peoples around 2,000 BE and were probably aware of their constellational systems. Things changed after Alexander's conquest circa 330 BCE. Greek and Mesopotamian ideas began to permeate Egypt and the Babylonian constellations and the zodiac were gradually assimilated.

Why didn't the Egyptians use constellations before that? The reason is pretty simple. Constellations demarcate space and directions, so they're useful for navigation. Mesopotamian tribes were migratory herders, and the Phoenicians were marine navigators. They needed the sky to function as a map. In contrast, the Egyptians were sedentary agrarians that worked the fertile lands along the Nile

River. They didn't need a map. They used the sky as a clock and a calendar, with the Sun and stars as temporal markers.

In the Egyptian cosmos, celestial movements were attributed to the divine magic of the Sun god Ra and Isis. As the Sun God moves, he turns the heavens and turns time. Turning time is the Ka-Soul of the Universe. The Sun personifies order and time as he steers the solar boat through the celestial waters day and night.

The word for star is "seba" (*sb3*) which means "the one who reveals form." The word seba contains "ba", the word for soul. The Egyptians believed that souls are stars and stars are souls. Each decan star was associated with a deity that shared its name, personality, characteristics, meanings, and functions with the decan.

Ba soul

Stars and souls share the same cyclic pathway. When a star rises with the Sun, it is the *First*. After the decan star's week is past, the star enters the *Lake of the Sky*. It's no longer visible because it's in the sky during the day. This phase of invisibility lasts about eighty days. When the decan star becomes visible at night, it is *Born*. The newborn star enters the *Lake of the Duat*, the night sky, and undergoes a purification process. Souls go through the same process after death: an invisible journey through the sky into the Duat (the night sky), where it is purified before entering the afterlife.

Anthropologist Joanne Conman[1] investigated the Egyptian contribution to ancient astrology and the Egyptian decan star system. Her hypothesis is that decan stars worked in pairs. Different stars are named on different lists. Demetra George[2] has also focused her attention on the decan lists and identifies at least three or more separate decan lists created over several centuries. Revisions in the decan stars and deities were inevitable during the 2,600 or more years that this system was in use. The last identifiable decan list exchanges stars for images—that is, the Face images. There are documented upheavals in Egyptian's religious beliefs that could have impacted the star lore.

The sacred secrets of the decan stars were not a part of early Alexandrian-Hellenic astrology. Accessible Egyptian celestial knowledge and philosophy provided the basis for house meanings. The final Ptolemaic dynasty was of Macedonian-Greek origin and put into place after Alexander the Great conquered Egypt. Sacred knowledge wasn't shared with non-natives.

The magically moving sky of the Egyptians is at odds with the ideas found in the celestial mechanics conceptualized in Greek philosophy. The elaborate assignments of deity-related stars to decans were eventually replaced with planet attributions in Chaldean order. The Faces (or decans) have very little importance in traditional astrology. The signs, triplicities, and bounds take precedence over the faces, which are at the bottom of dignity pecking order.

Egyptian Time

Egyptians had complex concepts about time and different ways of measuring it. The main calendrical measurement was the *unut* (*wnwt*), a ten-day week governed by a heliacal rising star—the decan star and its deity. When the star rose with the Sun, the deity associated with the star was said to "walk the Earth."

Neheh time was connected to the Sun God Ra and Seth (Mercury). It's roughly equivalent to linear time, as it is chaotic, ever-flowing time that distinguishes the collective experience of time passages.

Set and Ra with djedd, after an ancient Egyptian carving. EH

Djet time is associated with Osiris, the dead god. It emphasizes the duration of a particular event that continues to produce a field of cause-and-effect. Things flow from, and link back to, a fixed point in the past. Many events create overlapping vectors that continue to generate effects. Djet time is the conceptual basis for birth charts, and the idea that sky-related fate and destiny are conferred at birth. The moment of birth confers causes-and-effects through life.

The djet or djedd glyph symbolizes the spine of Osiris. It's a vertical column with horizontal bars that depicts power rising from the earth to the heavens. The djet was a ladder or cosmic conduit for the ba-souls of the dead to ascend into the pathways of the afterlife, and likewise a conduit for deities and souls to return to Earth. The path into the afterlife was described in several ways, including a golden rope, a ladder, a stairway, and through the flight of the soul.

Djet

The Egyptians also had the concept of *zep tepi*, which means "the first time." *Zep tepi* gave authority to religion, magic, medicine, and the directional orientation of buildings. The original *zep tepi* marked the first stirring of the High God in the Primeval Waters, as Horus accepted his throne and Osiris was redeemed. *Zep tepi* was the beginning of time itself, and the progenitor of djet time.[3]

Sothic Cycles

Earth's year contains 365 ¼ days. Every fourth year a "leap day" is added to compensate for the annual quarter day. The Egyptians developed Sothic Cycles, a method of long-term time accounting that calculates the quarter-day drift over time. This creates a cycle of 365 ¼ x 4, or 1,461 years. The start of a new Sothic Cycle is regenerative and signals a cultural awakening. It's associated with the rebirth of Bennu Bird, the Egyptian phoenix, much like the beginning of the Mayan Long Count is dominated by Quetzalcoatl, another fabulous bird god.

New Sothic cycles were characterized by dramatic religious reforms, intellectual and creative changes. If a new cycle started during the lifetime of a pharaoh, he was empowered to make enormous changes. Censorinus, a Roman writer in the 3rd century CE, recorded that the most recent Sothic Cycle started on July 21st Julian (June 25 Gregorian) in 139 AD. From this we can extrapolate years when new Sothic Cycles began: 11,451 BC, 10,081 BC, 8621 BC, 7160 BC, 5701 BC, 4241 BC, 2781 BC, 1321 BC. In the current era: 139 CE, 1600 CE, and 3061 CE.

Egyptologists Robert Bauval and Dr. Thomas Brophy have developed a theory that the original *zep tepi* was the Summer Solstice in 11,451 BC. Their astronomical software shows that this is when the Sirius first rose with the Sun at the latitude of Giza. Carbon-dated evidence from Nabta Playa appears to substantiate this extremely early date. Bauval and Brophy argue that the Paleolithic migratory herders of the Gebel Uwainat (or Jebel Uweinat), the currently uninhabitable mountain region southwest of Egypt's western desert where Nabta Playa is located, are the progenitors of the Egyptian civilization and the original collectors of Egyptian star lore. This region was wet and fertile but eventually turned into a desert. The natives migrated northward into the Nile Valley, where water was plentiful, and brought their star-lore with them.

Although Bauval and Brophy are criticized by other Egyptologists, the earliest funerary texts and art include a great deal of complex celestial information. This knowledge came from *somewhere*. The earliest accepted date for Egyptian civilization is 3,100 BCE, but accumulated celestial knowledge may well have been transmitted from earlier peoples who migrated into the region.

Transmigration of Souls

The Egyptians depicted ba-souls as human-headed birds that fly into the sky after death. The movement of ba-souls after death was connected with and timed by the stars. Pyramids were reincarnation machines that provided deceased pharaohs with the hardware and software necessary for the journey of the ba-soul through the dangerous pathways of the Duat. Like the phases of stars, ba-souls arrived in the afterlife with the rising Sun at the proper time.

The Step Pyramid at Saqqara is one of the oldest major construction sites in Egypt. It was designed and built by Imhotep for King Djoser around 2,600 BCE. The Saqqara pyramid is an architectural representation of the tripartite Egyptian cosmos with the Earth sandwiched between the Lake of Sky and the Lake of the Duat. A north-facing portal allowed the pharaoh's ba-soul to fly toward the northern skies on the beginning of its after-life journey.

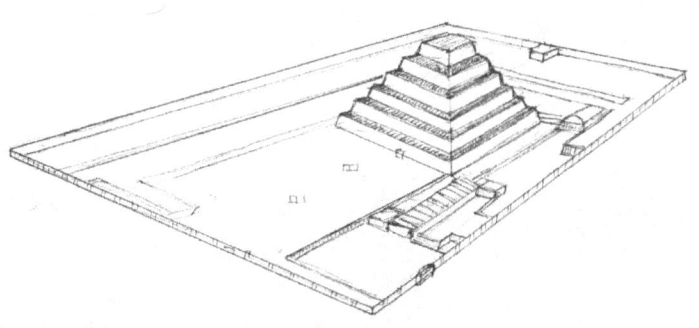

Model of the Step Pyramid at Saqqara

Chapter 2 The Egyptian Cosmos

The ultimate purpose of soul travel was to become *akh,* a spiritualized being. When a ba-soul exits the body of deceased, it enters the Duat and undergoes a purification process. When its journey is completed, the ba-soul rises before the Sun, gaining power and becoming effective—becoming *akh*. The times of human births and deaths were linked with the rising and setting decan stars, and the stars conferred fate, benefits and dangers.

The Hermit ibis was the hieroglyphic symbol for akh

The reddish glow in the east an hour or so before sunrise was called the *Akhet*. It's a zone of passage, a place of becoming effective, a cosmic combustion chamber capable of triggering rebirth and/or transubstantiation. The ba-soul is transformed into a newly effective *akh* mode of existence. The **Pyramid Text**[4] says: The king "becomes *akh* in the *Akhet*." The pharaoh's *akh* spirit continued to watch over and protect the people of Egypt in this form and could communicate with the gods on their behalf.

It is important to distinguish that the Akhet is *not* the horizon, but region just below the eastern horizon at dawn. The Sun, planets, stars, and souls are regenerated & reborn as *akhs*—spiritualized beings or light spirits—when they rise just before the Sun.

The concept of a cosmic combustion chamber just below the eastern horizon is the source of the idea of an Ascendant and first house in a birth chart. The soul gets a body and becomes effective. Other house meanings are derived from Egyptian concepts about fate and fortune as conferred by the gods at birth.

Stars and planets rise in the pre-dawn glow.

The Ahket is the cosmic combustion chamber just below the eastern horizon

Chapter 3

The Mesopotamian Cosmos

Mesopotamia is known as the Cradle of Civilization or the Fertile Crescent. A chain of cities were built between two substantial rivers, the Tigres and the Euphrates. Mesopotamia hosted several different kingdoms: the Sumerians, Akkadians, Hitittes, and Babylonians, and others. One tribe dominated the area for a while and then was overthrown by another tribe. The Babylonians became dominant around 1,900 BCE, and fell in 1,499 BCE. The great Persian empire of Darius and Xerxes eventually developed in the area, and was conquered by Alexander the Great in the 330s BCE.

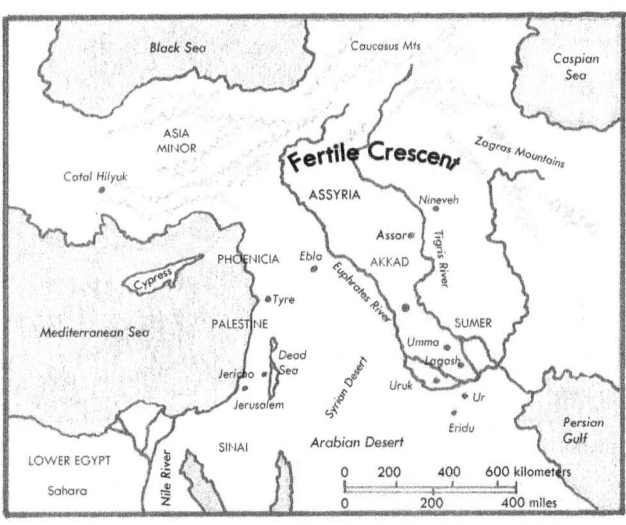

Map of Ancient Mesopotamia and the Sumerian Empire 5000 BCE to 2000 BCE. EH

The early empires of the Middle East were neighbors to the Egyptians. The Sinai Peninsula gave access for trade, migration, and wars along with cultural and religious exchanges. The cosmological concepts and star-based religions of these separate cultures had similarities but were not identical.

Information was passed down in Mesopotamia, but not as consistently as it was in Egypt. The ancient Middle East was home to many diverse migratory herding tribes. Egypt was a distinct culture by 3,100 BCE. It continued to exist even after Cleopatra was defeated by the Romans in 33 BCE. Egyptian royal dynasties came and went over the centuries, but the Nile Valley culture was sustained in mostly uninterrupted continuity for nearly 3,500 years. The five-hundred or so years of the Babylonian empire is dinky in comparison.

The Sumerians were the first great culture of Mesopotamia. A great deal of Mesopotamian star lore, mythology, and magic has Sumerian roots. The Mesopotamian Cosmos consists of layers of realms. The outer-most sky realm belonged to Anu, the god who created the cosmos, set it in motion, and withdrew to the uppermost skies. Beneath Anu's realm was the realm of the Igigi, the gods and goddesses of their divine pantheon. Beneath this was the realm of Heavenly Bodies, the planets and constellations, which the Igigi controlled and used to exert influence on people and events. The earthly plane was divided into quadrants that correspond to the cardinal directions. Beneath the Earth's surface was the realm of the Apsu, a watery realm that hosted sages, a few water deities, and a race of merpeople. This makes sense for a culture that was contained between two rivers that empty into the Persian Gulf. At the very bottom was the Underworld, the realm of the dead. (see diagram, facing page)

An invisible stairway connects everything from the Realm of the Igigi to the Underworld. It is the means for human souls and gods to travel between these realms. The stair-step construction of ziggurats in this region mimics the idea of a stairway to heaven. If the Tower of Babel actually existed, it was built with this kind of design.

Egyptian Serqet (above) and Scorpion goddess Ishara-tam-tim on green jasper Greco-Phoencian amulet.

Constellations were developed by the peoples of Mesopotamia. They conceived images in arrangements of stars, and attached stories and characteristics to them. They devised the Zodiac, a group of star images mostly contained in the ecliptic, the central band of sky where the Sun and planets travel. The ancient bird constellations Cygnus and Aquila were associated with soul movement. Like Egyptian ba-souls, the Mesopotamians believed that souls took wing to fly to the afterlife.

They were aware of the Galactic Center and thought it was the location of Paradise, the abode of souls in the afterlife. Getting there involved a dangerous journey through perilous terrain that was the stomping ground of horrible monsters. The portal to the Galactic Center was guarded by a Scorpion Goddess called Ishara-tam-tim. In Egypt, this goddess was called Serqet or Selket.

The Metaphysical Cosmos ✳ 15

The Mesopotamian Cosmos. EH

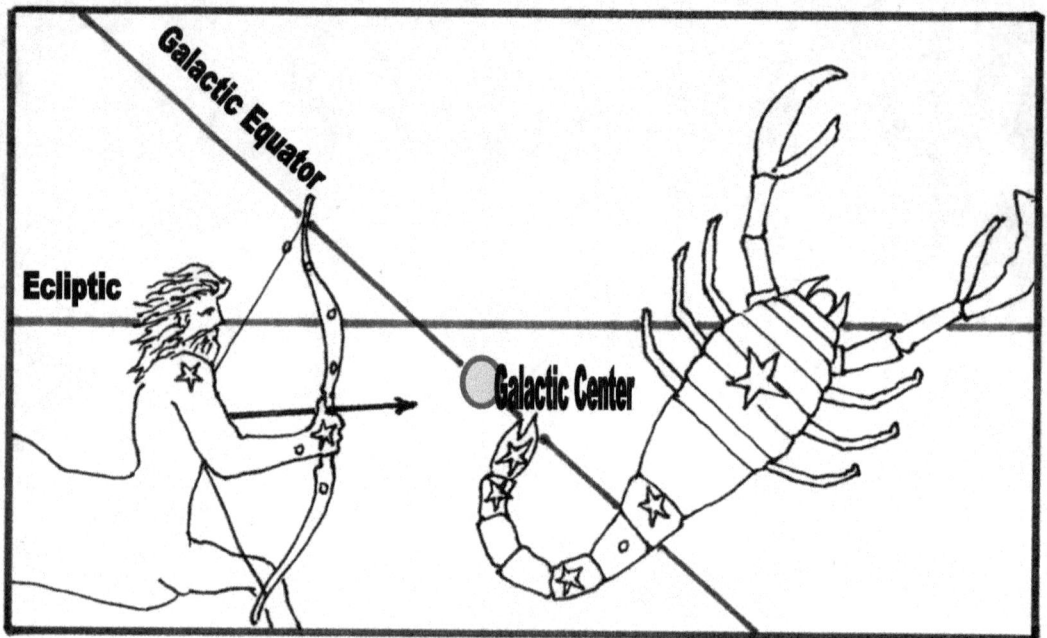

The Galactic Center is surrounded by the curve of the Scorpion's tail. The stars of the tail and stinger are associated with dangers, poisons, diseases/infections, all modes of death. Transmigrating souls had to get past all of these dangers to enter Paradise. Egyptian sources relate similar dangers on the path to the afterlife.

The Babylonian Catastrophe: Who Moved My Cheese?
Earth-Sun cycles are very stable. Day and night are equal at the Spring and Autumn equinoxes, and the Sun "turns" at the summer and winter solstices. These four annual events reflect earth's orbital cycle around the Sun, and this *never changes*.

Fixed stars aren't exactly fixed. They move very slowly, roughly one degree every seventy two years. Mesopotamians associated particular constellations with the solstices and equinoxes. Over time these stars drifted. Some kind of battle was taking place in the sky—the deities of the axis points were being overthrown! This was catastrophic. How could souls move into the afterlife if the gods that were responsible for this transition were no longer guarding the portals?

The problem had to be fixed. New constellations were devised along with new story-myths to explain the heavenly battles and the new portal guardian deities. The ecliptic zodiacal constellations that appeared around the critical solstices and equinoxes were reconfigured. Some of the constellations outside of the ecliptic remained intact. This "Zodiac 2.0" was devised around 500 BCE. The Greeks of the Aegean Islands and Alexandria in Egypt used Zodiac 2.0 when they developed astrology, and this is the zodiac that we're still using. For those interested in further study on this topic, Gavin White's book, **Babylonian Star-Lore**,[1] explores the earlier constellations of Zodiac 1.0.

Constellations are not permanent or static! Earth-dwellers have to stay on top of celestial housekeeping if their societies use the sky as a clock, as a map, and as a source of fate and fortune. This is especially important for constellations at the solstices, as these are entwined with beliefs about the transmigration of souls.

Ancient Astronomical Knowledge

There's no precise date for the development of astrology. Evidence suggests it was developed somewhat prior to the time of Alexander the Great's conquests, circa 300 BCE. Early astrologers were still familiar with some of the constellations from Zodiac 1.0. A partial list of earlier constellations is included at the end of **Rhetorius the Egyptian**[2] (translated by James Hershel Holden; the star list is from Porphyry's *Commentary on Antiochus*, a text that's been lost).

There are misapprehensions about what was known or unknown about the cosmos in ancient times.

◆ Some people knew that Earth orbits the Sun. In the 3rd century BCE, Aristarchus of Samos proposed a Sun-centered system. He noted that Sun-related Earth dates, the equinoxes and solstices, remain consistent even when stars move. Diodorus Siculus (1st c BCE) wrote that the Chaldeans used a Sun-centered system. Claudius Ptolemy, the author-compiler of **Tetrabiblos**,[3] either wasn't aware of this information or chose not to include it. He used an earth-centered system that remained the standard until a sun-centered system was proposed by Copernicus and vetted by Galileo.

◆ The ancients knew that stars move. In the 2nd century BCE, Hipparchus wrote about the Precession of the Equinoxes. The Greeks were avid travelers and information collectors. Mesopotamia and Egypt were well within their program of tourism, and both cultures had long traditions of star-watching. Without a doubt, the slow apparent movement of fixed stars was known.

◆ Pythagoras suggested that the Earth was round circa 500 BCE based on empirical reasoning. By 430 BCE, Anaxagoras figured out what caused solar and lunar eclipses, and noted that the Earth cast a round shadow on the face of the Moon. Aristotle confirmed that notion through his own observations around 350 BCE. Over the next one hundred years, Aristarchus and Eratosthenes attempted to calculate the Earth's diameter.

By the time of Alexander the Great, people were aware that stars move, and that Earth rotates around the Sun, and that Earth is a sphere. Why didn't these facts survive or get passed along into the Middle Ages?

Titus Burchardt,[4] a mid-20th century scholar of ancient literature, suggested that the ancients valued experiential truths more than scientific facts. Anyone who watches the sky during the day can clearly see the Sun moving across the sky. At least, that's what we see. The night sky gives the same visual evidence of the stars and planets. Celestial objects appear to move, not Earth.

Even when contemporary astrologers refer to the "stars moving," it's a shorthand expression for "the apparent movement of the stars." Because, of course, the stars don't move. The Earth moves, the solar system moves, and the Milky Way galaxy rotates. We're a part of a massive universe filled with moving parts. The Earth's twenty-four hour rotation creates the optical effect of solar motion, and Earth's orbital cycle creates the visual impression that the Sun rises with a succession of constellations. Earth's wobbling axis gives the effect of stellar precession.

Burchardt's insightful position on the matter is that the ancients were more concerned with the human experience of the cosmos, not the facts of how it worked. The scientific fact of a Sun-centered system contradicts what human eyes see every day. What happens when you tell someone that what they see isn't real? It creates distrust in basic sense perceptions. If the visual "truth" about the Sun's movement across the sky isn't true, what else are are people getting wrong?

The ancient Mesopotamians, Egyptians, and Greeks believed that the sky was a place where gods lived. This divine realm was the source of fate and fortune. Numbers were sacred, too. Music, math, and sky lore were interrelated. That was their truth about the sky. Humans and human souls had a direct relationship to the stars, and the Sun and Moon were divine orbs that regulated life on Earth. Earth and sky were interconnected, and souls made a great circuit of life back and forth along cosmic pathways. The mysteries surrounding life and death and the journey of human souls were more important than facts about the cosmos.

The intellectual priorities of the ancient world are very different than those of the world we occupy. Burchardt posed the very relevant question: does awareness of the Sun-centered system offers any real improvement to the lives of the vast majority of humans? Western astrologers use the Earth-centered or geocentric tropical zodiac system. We don't live on the Sun or watch the solar system from that vantage point. Celestial movements are viewed from Earth, the third rock from the Sun. Birth charts are cast from the location of birth on Earth. The benefits and liabilities of scientific facts are worth more than a casual nod, especially from astrologers.

I'm a geocentric astrology geek and a science geek. It's an intellectual paradox, but I'm aware that it's a paradox and have learned how to live with it. To me, Burchardt's question is best addressed by letting people know, up front, that they're being told facts that are contrary to apparent phenomena. People seem to develop better coping skills when they understand that being human involves accepting irresolvable paradoxes.

Chapter 4
Changes in Cosmic Time

The term Western astrologers use to describe the great cycle of the cosmos is the **Precession of the Equinoxes**. A **Great Year** or **Platonic Year** is 25,772 solar years in length. The **Platonic Year** is divided by twelve zodiac signs, creating twelve **Platonic Months** of 2,150 years. The Platonic Month is further divided by twelve, resulting in a **Platonic Day,** which is 179 years long. A Platonic Day is equal to a Great Mutation, the pattern that Jupiter and Saturn as they form conjunctions in a single element for roughly 180 years before they shift into another element.

A Platonic Month is also called an **Age**, an **Aeon** or **Aion**. A new age begins when a new zodiacal constellation begins to rise with the Sun at Spring Equinox, which is 0° Aries in the tropical, Earth-centric zodiac. The stars appear to move backwards very slowly, so the Age of Aries was followed by the current Age of Pisces. The Age of Pisces is followed by the Age of Aquarius, then the Age of Capricorn, and so on. Spring Equinox is "the Aries Point" in tropical astrology, and is the fiducial (starting) point of the zodiac.

Celestial fiducial points are a human device. A year can begin at any time, but throughout recorded history, most civilizations have selected a culturally-appropriate fiducial point or New Year's date. The four notable moments in a solar year—the two equinoxes and two solstices—are logical selections. The Egyptians chose the Sun's rising with the star Sirius as their fiducial point. For many centuries, Sirius rose with the Sun at the same time as the Nile flooded, but eventually the star's apparent movement eroded the synchronicity of the two events. From a religious and cultural standpoint, this was cataclysmic. Other global cultures have floundered because particular holy dates have been associated with the appearance of certain stars at dawn or dusk, and this leads to havoc when the star's position changes. Linking the start of a new year to one of the equinoxes or solstices is guaranteed to last and is a safer cultural investment.

There are other options. The Chinese and other Asian cultures begin the new year on the New Moon in Aquarius (tropical). The Roman New Year started in February, too. Diwali, the Hindu New Year, is celebrated at the New Moon in Scorpio. Using a lunation to signify a new year results in a floating holiday; the date changes from year to year. China and India adopted the Gregorian calendar and use January 1st as a significant business date while retaining their traditional lunar New Year dates for cultural celebratory purposes. Various cultures sustain a Moon-based ritual calendar alongside the globally-accepted Gregorian calendar. The only Moon-based Christian ritual date is Easter, which is the first Sunday after the Full Moon after Spring Equinox (the Full Moon in Libra).

Wiccans and many neo-pagans use Samhain (Halloween, October 31st) as their New Year. It is the midpoint between Mabon (Autumn Equinox) and Yule (Winter Solstice), also called a cross-quarter date. Beginning the pagan New Year at the end of autumn is similar in concept to the Jewish tradition of using sundown as the beginning of a day.

People who make and fail to keep New Year's resolutions should be happy to discover that there are at least a half-dozen recognized New Years during a calendar year.

Aeon Calculations

In the 1980s Rob Hand, Zip Dobbyns, and Mark Pottenger created software to calculate the precession of the equinoxes.[1]

Age of Taurus:	4143 B.C. to 1695 B.C.
	(159 *year overlap*)
Age of Aries:	1854 B.C. to 389 B.C.
	(279 *year gap*)
Age of Pisces:	110 B.C. to **2817 C.E.**
	(126 *year overlap*)
Age of Aquarius:	**2691 to 5431 C.E.**
	(1012 *year overlap*)
Age of Capricorn:	4419 to 6068 C.E.

The calculations extend through the Age of Gemini in 18, 675 CE. Neil Mann compiled a set of calculations based on the Platonic Months:

Age of Taurus:	4300 BCE to 2150 BCE
Age of Aries:	2150 BCE to 1 CE
Age of Pisces:	1 CE to 2150 CE
Age of Aquarius:	2150 CE to 4300 CE

Mann's list ignores overlapping constellations and gap periods. The 20th-century British astrologer Charles Carter stated that "It is probable that there is no branch of Astrology upon which more nonsense has been poured forth than the doctrine of the precession of the equinoxes."[2] Nicholas Campion collected over 90 dates provided by researchers for the start of the Age of Aquarius. The range of dates for the possible beginning of the Aquarian Age range from 1447 to 3621. The Austrian astronomer Hermann Haupt published an article in 1992 based on the constellational boundaries accepted by the International Astronomical Union (IAU) in 1928. According to his research, the Aquarian Age will begin in 2595.

The contention around these Aeon dates have something to do with the glitches of the groovy Greek math that divides the zodiac into tidy little 30-degree sign segments, and Platonic Months into tidy 2150-year intervals. If calculations are based on the actual size of constellations, the duration of aeons is unequal because the zodiacal constellations are different sizes. Some constellations overlap, and some are very small and leave empty spaces between star groups.

Pisces is a huge constellation, so in the calculations made by Hand, Dobbyns and Pottenger, the transition from the Age of Pisces to the Age of Aquarius has 126-year overlap. The team's estimate of the Aquarian Age beginning in 2691 CE is only 100 years off from Haupt's calculation of 2595 CE. This contrasts with Neil Mann's calculations, which simply assigns aeons to 2150-year segments prescribed by the divisions of the Ptolemaic Year.

The date of the anticipated shift to the Aquarian Age is of less concern for the purposes of this text than the anticipated impact of an Aeon shift. That was an important topic of focus for De Santillana and Von Dechend in **Hamlet's Mill**. According to their research, the ending of an Aeon is characterized by deterioration and corruption. New Aeons are associated with massive cultural changes, typically characterized by transformed religions and new gods. As part of this process, there are changes in the meanings of symbols, transformations of political and economic systems, and intellectual changes. The collective systems and standards by which human civilizations exist are transformed. The key phrase identified in **Hamlet's Mill** is "weights and measures." The effect is collective, not individual, because this takes hundreds of years to happen. Rome wasn't built in a day, and it didn't fall down overnight, either.

I recommend two books on the effects of Aeon changes. **Aion**[3] by Carl Jung discusses how the meanings of symbols change and transform. Symbols are extremely persistent through human history but the meaning of symbols changes over several centuries and through use by different cultural groups. **American Gods**[4] by Neil Gaiman is one of the most important books of the first decade of the 21st century. It is a fictional work that aptly describes the clash between old gods and new gods, and suggests how collective cultures give power to new gods. It also depicts how old gods can adapt and survive into new eras.

North Star Shifts

In addition to the great cycle of zodiacal precession, a second major celestial phenomenon is the shifting of the North Star. Like Aeons, North Stars change through a 26,000-year cycle that doesn't coincide with Aeon shifts. The North Star is a point of cosmic stasis, so changes in the past have been catastrophic from a religious and cultural standpoint.

Plato wrote that the North Star was attached to Earth by a golden chain or cord, and it leads the Earth through the sky. When the North Star shifts, the earth's relationship with the galaxy is thrown into chaos. The North Star changes at irregular intervals. (see diagram on following page)

The golden chain between Earth and the North Star. EH

Vega (Lyra) 12,000 BCE – 3000 BCE

Thuban (Draco) 3000 BCE – 1900 BCE

Kochab (Ursa Minor) 1900 BCE – 1100 BCE

Polaris (Ursa Minor) 1100 BCE – 7500 C.E.

Alderamin (Cepheus) 7500-10,000 C.E.

Deneb Adige (Cygnus) 10,000 – 14,000 C.E.

Vega (Lyra) 14,000 - ? C.E.

Vivian Robson equated the North Star cycles with a full cycle of Aeons. He wrote: "The chief stars that will mark the position of the pole are successively as follows—γ, π, ζ, ν, and α Cephei; α and δ Cygni; α Lyrae; ι and τ Herculis; Θ, ι, and α Draconis; β Ursae Minoris, our Polaris. About the year 12,200 BC, α Lyrae (Wega) marked the pole; ι Draconis about 4,500 BC; and α Draconis about 2,700 BC, while γ Cephei will occupy this position in about 4,500 AD; α Cephei in 7,500 AD; δ Cygni in 11,300 AD; and Wega in about 13,500 AD." [5]

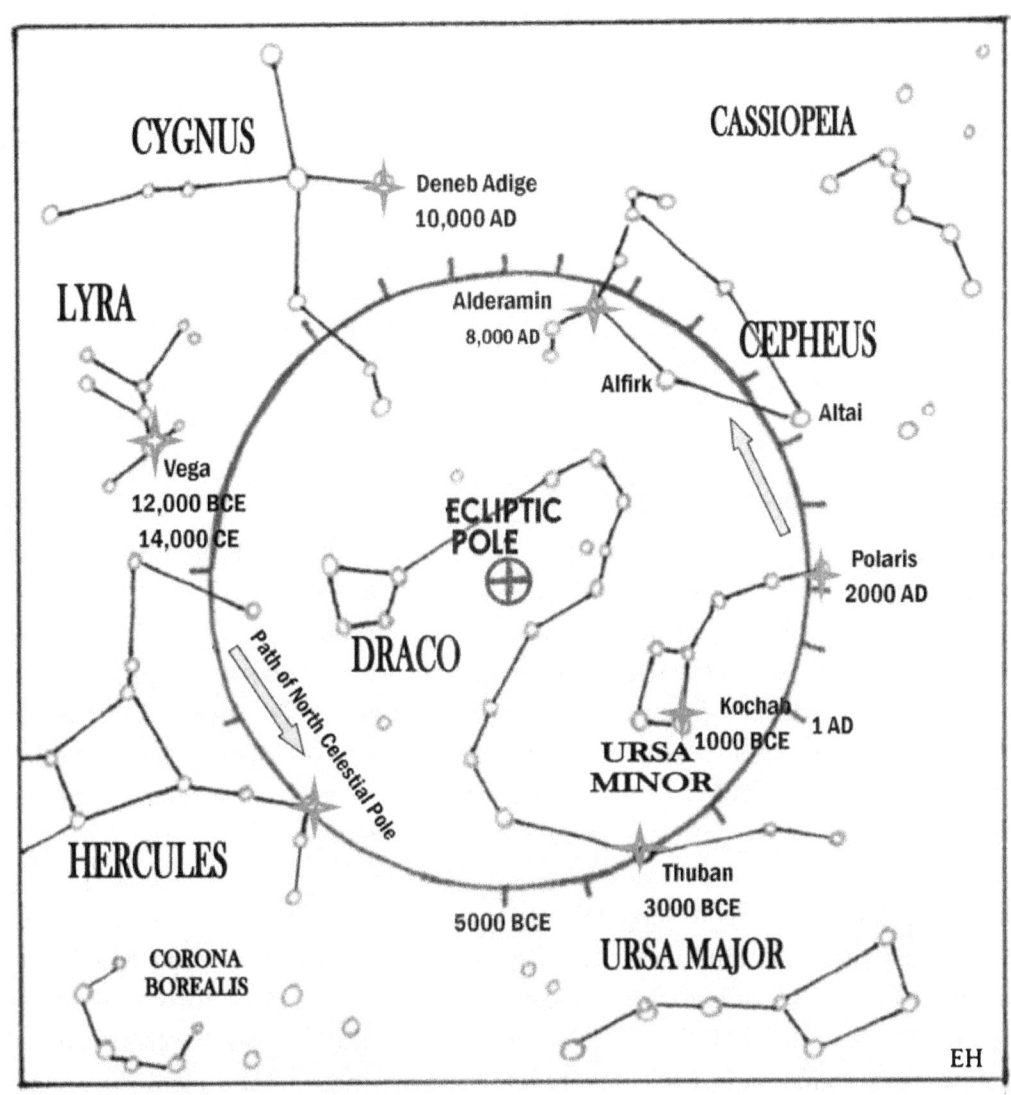

North Star Shifts from 12,000 BCE to 14,000 CE

Vega (alpha Lyra) is the North Star connected with the Golden Age, which would have coincided with the Age of Leo. This is a lucky star that relates to music and the arts, and as a North Star it is associated with peaceful civilizations. Gobekli Tepi and Nabta Playa were constructed when Vega began its role as the North Star.

Iota and alpha Draconis (Thuban) were the North Stars when the "Neolithic package" of skills sets and agricultural developments were slowly spreading throughout the ancient world. The Neolithic Package is an archeological term for a collection of developing human skills that include agriculture, herding, weaving, and pottery production. Kochab became the North Star as Egypt and a succession of empires in Mesopotamian grew powerful, and was due north at the "invasions of the Sea Peoples." This focal event in ancient history was part of a series of upheavals, terrible droughts, earthquakes, climate changes, and invasions that badly disrupted international relationships and trade routes of the ancient world around the Mediterranean circa 1,100-1,000 BCE. North Stars and their changes are not viewed kindly.

Polaris is the current North Star and it is not a good one. The meanings of Polaris are dark and violent. Polaris will reach true celestial North in 2,095 CE.

The Twirling Milky Way

One thing cannot be emphasized enough about ancient peoples: ideas were inspired by *what people could see*. Stone Age sites are oriented to celestial phenomenon: what people saw the sky inspired them to build in stone. Transporting a 60-ton megalith twenty miles requires immense man-power, and this effort was repeated hundreds of times over hundreds of years. The human cost is staggering, yet people in ancient communities constructed dozens of stone circles and other structures. What did they see that generated such intense, long-term dedication to the construction of stone structures on such an immense scale?

Stone Age social and technological changes were regional, slow, and sporadic. Some areas, like Britain, were late to absorb changes but progressed more quickly after developments from the continent were integrated into their society. The Stone Age is divided into the Paleolithic, Mesolithic, and Neolithic periods. Rudimentary forms of writing developed in the middle of the Neolithic period. Writing and record-keeping were well established in some areas as the Bronze Age began. The Stone Age was predominantly pre-literate, so studies rely on stone structures and artifacts.

This requires a caveat: conclusions about Stone Age sites and artifacts involve speculation. A great deal of independent confirmation is required before archeological speculations are accepted in the field's scholarly mainstream. Mass-spectral analysis, carbon-dating, satellite imaging, DNA analysis, and astronomical software have had a huge impact on archeology in the past few decades. Some of the conclusions presented below are relatively new and may not be widely accepted as yet; however, new theories in development by archeo-astronomers merit the attention of astrologers.

Paleolithic Age - 11,000 to 5,000 BCE: The Paleolithic Age spread slowly from the epicenter in the Fertile Crescent into Europe and the British Isles. It was the transition from tribal hunter-gathering to migratory herding with some rudimentary agricultural practices. Growing evidence suggests a fairly sophisticated awareness of solar and lunar cycles and long-term star tracking practices.

♦ A section of the cave paintings in the **Salon des Taurees** in Lescaux, France has been identified as a star map of the sky at Summer Solstice circa 15,000 BCE.
♦ **Nabta Playa** (circa 11,500-6,100 BCE) is a mostly intact group of stone star markers at a site in southwest Egypt. The stones mark the slow-changing positions of Sirius and other stars tracked over thousands of years.
♦ **Gobekli Tepi** (circa 11,000 – 8,000 BCE) in what is now southern Turkey was a vast complex of carved stones probably used as a sacred site. The site was deliberately buried under thousands of tons of soil around 8,000 BCE. The reason for this is unknown. The progress on this site is worth watching, as evidence of star markers and construction oriented to sky phenomena will probably be discovered.

Neolithic Age - 5,000 to 2,000 BCE: During this period, small but stable, permanent communities formed in resource-rich areas, especially along river routes. The "Neolithic Package" was a range of skills that include farming, domesticated herd animals, pottery, stone working, spinning and weaving, rudimentary quarrying and mining of various types of stone, metal ores, and gemstones. These skills spread unevenly into different regions at different times. Timber markers on Paleolithic sites were gradually replaced with massive stone markers. Accumulating evidence suggests that Meso- and Neolithic peoples continued and expanded Paleolithic knowledge of Earth's relationship to celestial movements.

♦ **Goseck Henge** in Germany is one of the earliest stone circles. It was constructed circa 5,000 BCE. Stones replaced much earlier Paleolithic timber markers.
♦ **Avebury Henge Complex** in Britain features was a focal site from 8,000 BCE with overlapping phases of stone construction on eight major features from 4,000 to 2,200 BCE: the main stone henge with two inner circles; two long trails demarcated by standing stones; a long barrow; a gathering place at the end of the east trail; and a massive conical earth mound called Silberry Hill. An intense building program took place on the Avebury plain from 4,500 BCE. Timber markers were replaced with standing stones. Hundreds of standing stones formed a huge outer circle with two smaller inner circles. Two long stone-marked trails led into the circle from the north and east.

♦ The earliest trace evidence at **Stonehenge** dates to 3,400 BCE. Construction started in 3,000 BCE and was completed around 1,800 BCE.
♦ The **Step Pyramid at Saqarra** dates from 2,600 BCE and is a model of the tripartite cosmos. It was built on top of an earlier construction.

The Extraordinary Avebury Henge

Nicholas Mann has done extensive research into the massive Mesolithic-Neolithic stone structures around Avebury, a site that was in active use and constant construction for thousands of years. Carbon dating was used to identify when the earliest timber posts were set. An alternative method for dating the site is gauging the positions of the great stones and their relationship to ancient stellar rising and setting positions. *Redshift* and *Starry Night Pro* software programs were used to match up stones and stars.[6]

The builders weren't simply building a henge to track stars; they were replicating the cosmos on the surface of the Earth. Architectural earth-sky mirroring construction was done in Egypt, India, by the Mayans and later indigenous tribes, so this isn't an anomalous discovery. What's unusual about Avebury Henge is how its builders decided to mirror the sky and the elaborate design scheme they implemented over many centuries.

The Avebury Henge complex is remarkably special and different from Stonehenge. The critical features of the site include the position-markers for the stars at the time of Avebury's development and the utilitarian purposes of the stone circles. A comparison of these two sites underscores the changes in social development during the transition from Neolithic Avebury to Bronze Age Stonehenge.

Avebury is at a latitude of 51° North. Important southern stars and impressive asterisms (star groupings) were visible at this latitude around 8,000 BCE. The dynamic interaction of three properties of the cosmos produced dramatic visible combinations after 5,000 BCE. These include the Milky Way (the galactic equator), the solar system's ecliptic (path of the Sun, Moon and planets), and the slow wobble of earth's rotational axis.

The crossroads of the Milky Way and ecliptic were aligned due east/west and were visible in the sky at the spring and autumn equinoxes circa 4,500 BCE. Key southern constellations visible at Avebury's latitude were the Southern Cross (Acrux) and alpha and beta Centauri. These are some of the brightest stars in the sky. The distinctive Southern Cross asterism rose in visual opposition to Cygnus,

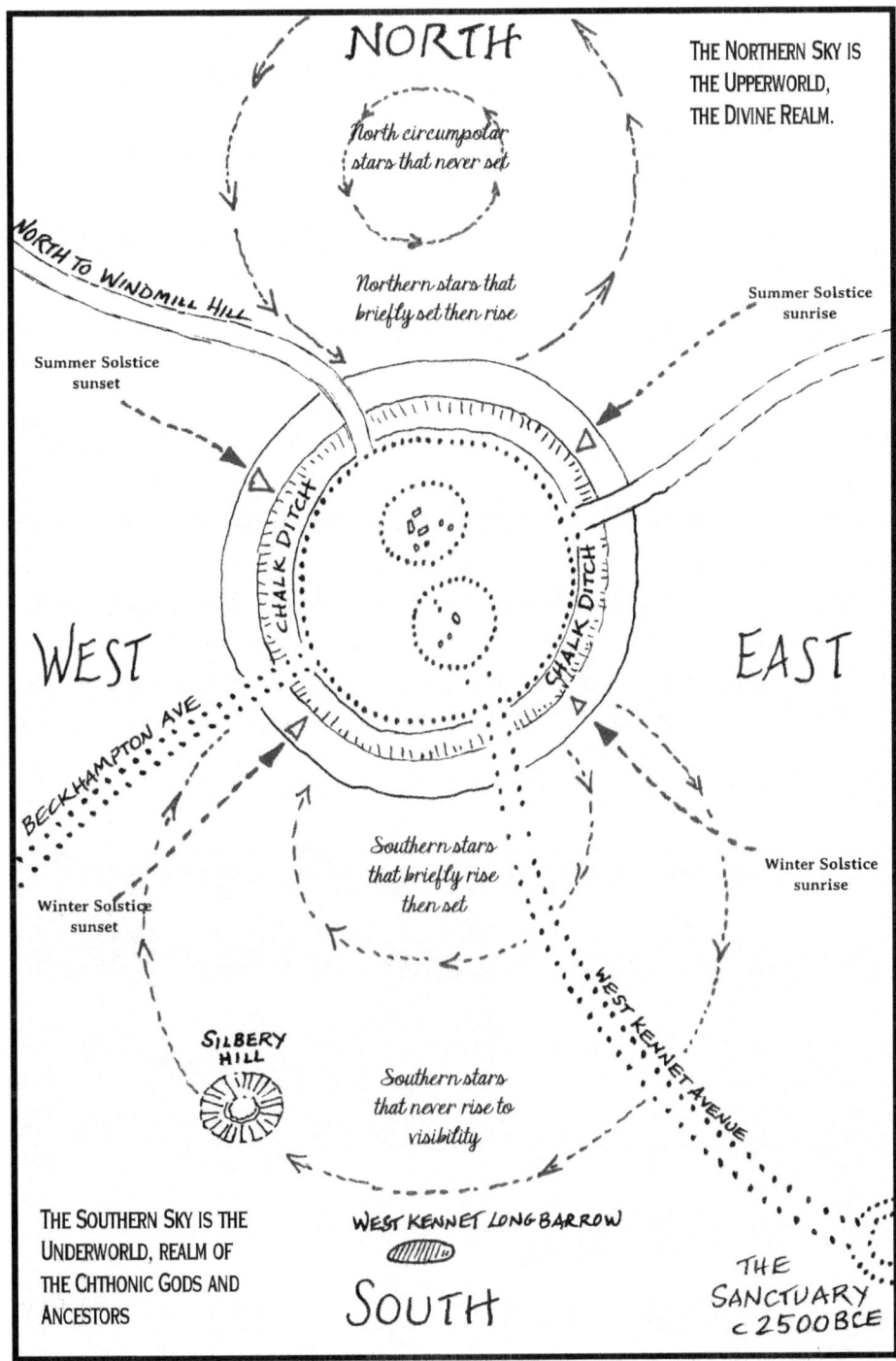

Overview of Avebury Henge, Wessex, England c 3250 to 2200 BCE

The outer circle is 360 yards in diameter with 100 stones. It is surrounded by a great ditch exposing the white chalk beneath the turf. The north inner circle has 27 stones and the south inner circle has 29 stones for tracking lunar cycles. The two circles contain central stones placed to track rising and setting stars. The paths leading into the circle symbolize the sky dragons—the ecliptic and galactic equator. West Kennet Avenue leads to the Sanctuary, an additional henge built around 2500 BCE. (drawing after Mann)

also known as the Northern Cross. Cygnus the Swan is one of the northern circumpolar constellations, while Acrux points toward the South Pole.

The Milky Way encircled the entire horizon at around 4:00 am on Winter Solstice with both Acrux and Cygnus visible *at the same time*. The visibility of the northern and southern crosses provided visual evidence of the cosmic axis or World Tree. The cosmos appeared to rotate around the earth with this axis at its center. The great circle of the Milky Way was replicated with a huge trench surrounding the outer stone circle. The chalk beneath the turf surface glowed white at night, especially when it was wet.

Within the white chalk trench and greater stone circle stood two smaller circles. One circle replicated the annual lunar cycle and the other circle the 18.5 year Metonic cycle. Individual stones inside of the small circles aligned to the rising and setting points of the North and South Crosses. Other stones marked the heliacal rising of Alnath at Beltane. Alnath, the horn of the Bull (beta Tauri), is the brightest star near the galactic anti-center, the intersection of the galactic equator and ecliptic. Another stone marked Alnath's acronychal (evening) setting at Samhain. Beltane and Samhain continue to be associated with birth and death.

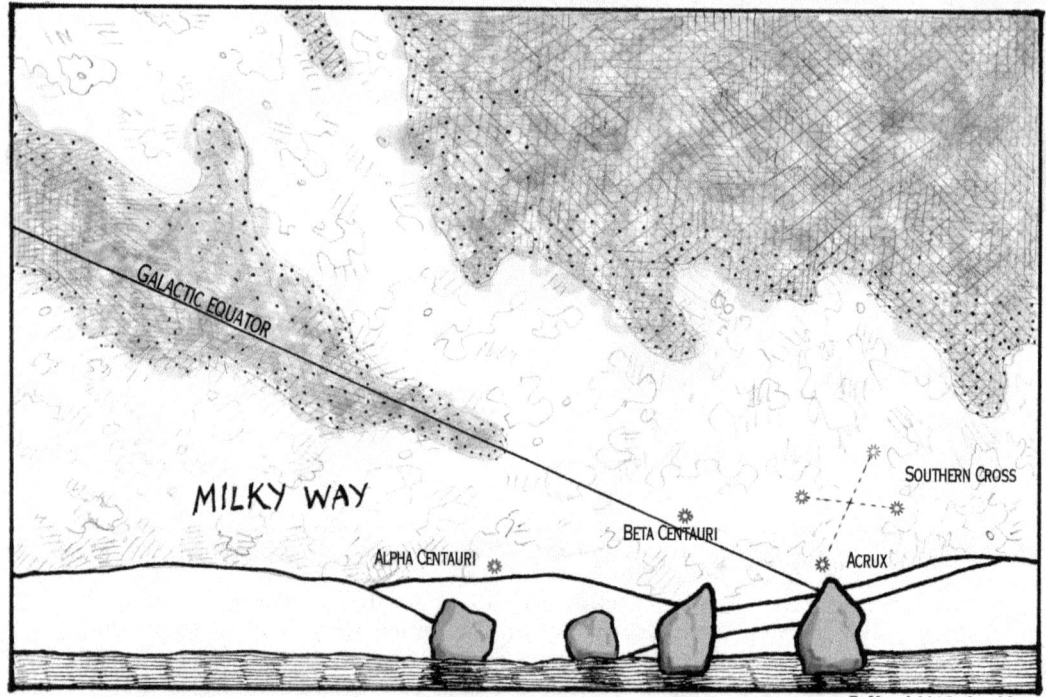

Southern stars sinking out of view. EH after Mann

The apparent motion of the cosmos has shifted through one quarter (6,500 years) of the 26,000 year Platonic Year cycle since 4,500 BCE. From the mid-1990s until the 2020s, the celestial crossroad once again aligned with the Summer and Winter Solstices, but at a right angle to it.

Dragon Wars
Many cosmological legends feature dragons. Geoffrey of Monmouth recorded a tale about King Vortigern and Merlin.[7] The King tried to construct a tower *but it kept sinking.* Merlin told him to dig down to a pool. The pool held a red and white dragon that fought bitterly, undermining the stability of the land. Mann writes that "...Celtic legends are emphatic that the two dragons should not come into conflict, or fall out of balance. Stability must be maintained, and the legends make it clear that humans can intervene in support of this...It is important firstly, to ensure that they are not in conflict, and secondly, that they are in the right place...their rightful position at the most powerful place: the centre of the land."

The Avebury complex features two long stone-lined avenues leading into the great circle. The builders completed West Kennet and Beckhampton Avenues around 2,300 BCE, just as Acrux and Centauri were sinking from view. The red and white dragons (avenues) are metaphors for the two great celestial circles: the Milky Way and the ecliptic. "...(T)he concern of the builders was to try to maintain or correct the balance of their monuments and the Poles, especially as the stars departed from their rightful position in the sky...to help in holding axial Dragons in place, even as they were being thrown alarmingly off balance by the cycle of precession." (See drawing, page 30)

A change in the heavens meant big changes on earth, and as Mann says, it was not good news.

The Milky Way began to tilt out of alignment with the earth's horizon. Mann believes that Silberry Hill, the enormous conical mound built from 2,500 to 2,300 BCE, was the final effort to keep these stars from sinking into the southern horizon. It didn't work. After 2,300 BCE, Acrux and Centaurus sank beneath the horizon and visibility. The Avebury complex and its comprehensive solar, lunar, and star markers fell into disuse.

The focus shifted to Stonehenge. This monument is primarily solar. The dolmens and lintels are arranged so that the sunrises and sunsets of the equinoxes and solstices are visible from within the circle. The Neolithic focus on the stars gave way to the Bronze Age focus on the Sun. It was a huge cultural shift away from the Avebury site's reflection of the celestial whole (animism, unity with nature, and collective cooperation) to Stonehenge's singular focus on a Sun god. Humans got the memo: the Sun's apparent position at the equinoxes and solstices is reliable, but star positions are not. Bronze Age Britain was dominated by regional tribal leaders who possessed enough status, wealth and manpower to challenge other tribes for the best land and natural resources.

The multi-level astronomical purposes and long-term development of Avebury describes the spirit of the Age of Taurus. Construction took one hundred generations of collective effort. Nomadic hunter-gathering-herding tribes evolved into a sedentary agrarian lifestyle, thus improving chances of stable food surpluses and population growth. Evidence suggests that large gatherings were conducted at Avebury in the autumn months after the harvesting season when there was plenty of food to store and share. The complex at Avebury was designed, built, modified and expanded over thousands of years.

What's even more significant is that the slight southern tilt of the Avebury plain produces an optical effect of speeding up precession. The normal visible rate of precession is roughly about 1 degree every 72 years. At Avebury this rate is increased to 1 degree every 25 years! The loss of the bright southern stars and the encircling Milky Way must have been dramatic and collectively devastating.

Stonehenge is a testament to the Age of Aries and the Bronze Age. Old British legends credit Merlin for the construction of Stonehenge, which was—in comparison to Avebury—built very quickly. That suggests leadership with enough wealth and power to make the stones "fly" from various sites to the new henge. The Sun is the star of the show and sole focus (pun intended). Standing stones for tracking the stars weren't included at this site, and only four dolmens track the Moon's most extreme positions (lunar stand-stills).

The abandonment of star- and Moon-tracking and the loss of sky lore from that period is distressing. Avebury Henge is an enormous site with multiple features. It required many people, perhaps long-established family groups passing information through oral traditions, to act as nightly watchers tracking celestial movements over many centuries. The watchers were probably considered priests and priestesses; their knowledge must have seemed magical to the uninformed.

Neolithic Britain was not a literate society. When use of the Avebury site ended, this unwritten lore was lost – perhaps. Verbal transmission is a remarkably persistent phenomenon. If contemporary Britains are any example, the peoples of this island are loathe to give up long-established traditions. Avebury was intact long after Stonehenge took precedence. Keepers dwelling near the Avebury site may have remained quietly dedicated to it for a long, long time. English nursery rhymes feature a character named Mother Goose. Who is she? The constellation Cygnus was seen as a goose in Britain. Perhaps some of their star wisdom has persisted disguised as children's rhymes and in fairy tales.

The Southern View
The early cities of Egypt are at the approximate latitude of 30° North. At this location during the Mesolithic period (4,000-2,000 BCE) the southernmost stars and constellations were visible, including Canopus, the Southern Cross, the stars of Eridanus (the river in the sky), Achernar (the mouth of the river), and the stars of Argo, the ship. In contrast, many of the northern circumpolar stars and star groups revolved above and below the northern horizon. The apparent rotation of the Helice (the helix, the northern circumpolar stars) was more dramatic. During the winter months, Cygnus was visible after sunset, flew beneath the northern horizon for several hours, then rose before the dawn. In summer, Cygnus flew above the Pole, then down toward the northern horizon, providing visible motion through the nocturnal hours. The circumpolar stars make one complete rotation in 24 hours, whereas the zodiacal stars on the ecliptic require a full year for an complete apparent orbital cycle.

Renenutet is the hippo-headed aspect of Isis. Gavin White describes the figure of Renenutet in the Zodiac of Dendera as "the hippo and the mooring post" in the circumpolar region.[8] The hippo goddess is next to a dog or wolf upon a plough. Isis-Renenutet assists the Sun god Ra's "strong arm" in turning the wheel of heavens. Bird-shaped ba souls enter the underworld as the constellation dips below the horizon. A bird constellation is near the dog's nose on the Dendera tondo.

"The Hippo and the Mooring Post" from the Zodiac of Dendera. EH

Isis is linked to two stars in different goddess forms. Isis-Renenutet occupied the Helice and the North Celestial Pole. Isis-Sepdet (Sirius) is the brightest star in the ecliptic, so it isn't much of a stretch to surmise that Isis-Renenutet has ties to Arcturus (alpha Boötes), the brightest star in the northern sky. A star near the celestial North Pole and another near the ecliptic helped Isis perform this time-turning magic. In somewhat similar fashion, the Mesopotamian constellation Šupa (Boötes), an avatar of Enlil, pushes the Ursa-plow to guide the destiny of nations and kings. Ursa Major as a plow is linked to the development and growing prominence of agriculture during the Age of Taurus. During the Age of Aries, Ursa Major was re-envisioned as a chariot, wagon, or a mama bear. Just as old gods get new jobs, old constellations get new images.

The Current View
The night skies of the habitable parts of the globe have changed quite dramatically in 6,500 years. The Milky Way currently bisects the Summer-Winter Solstice axis instead of *circling* the entire horizon as it did in 4,500 BCE. In another 6,500 years, circa 8,500 CE, the Milky Way will once again encircle the horizon at the Solstice but the stars will be in the opposite positions from those occupied in ancient times. Sagittarius will rise at Spring Equinox and Gemini will rise at Autumn Equinox. Northern stars will be almost directly overhead at Summer Solstice. Stars beneath the ecliptic will disappear from view in the northern hemisphere. Alderamin (Cepheus) will be the Pole Star.

The apparent motion of the stars is not just from west to east – the entire galaxy appears to shift over thousands of years. The rotational high point of the Avebury period (c 4,500 BCE) featured a spectacularly visible Cosmic Axis. We have lost sight of the Axis.

Ancient spiritual mythologies that merged the twirling celestial whole with Earth to form a layered, integrated cosmos have been set aside as antiquated curiosities and replaced with simplistic religious mythologies that entirely neglect the sky. Industrialized nations have only a few, residual celebrations that reflect cosmic time. Electric lights pollute the night so the stars aren't visible. Even clocks no longer have faces. Time has become digital and impersonal; it has lost all the vestiges of its sacred character. We are collectively poorer for the diminution of imaginative relationships to the sky and time.

Spring Equinox has barely begun to align with the stream of stars falling from the Water Bearer's jug. In ancient times these stars symbolized the rains that nourished bountiful crops and sustained all of Earth's creatures and plant growth. Wealth is concentrated in the hands of a few, and this is contrary to what the approaching Age of Aquarius and its life-giving stars signify.

The Metaphysical Cosmos ✵ 35

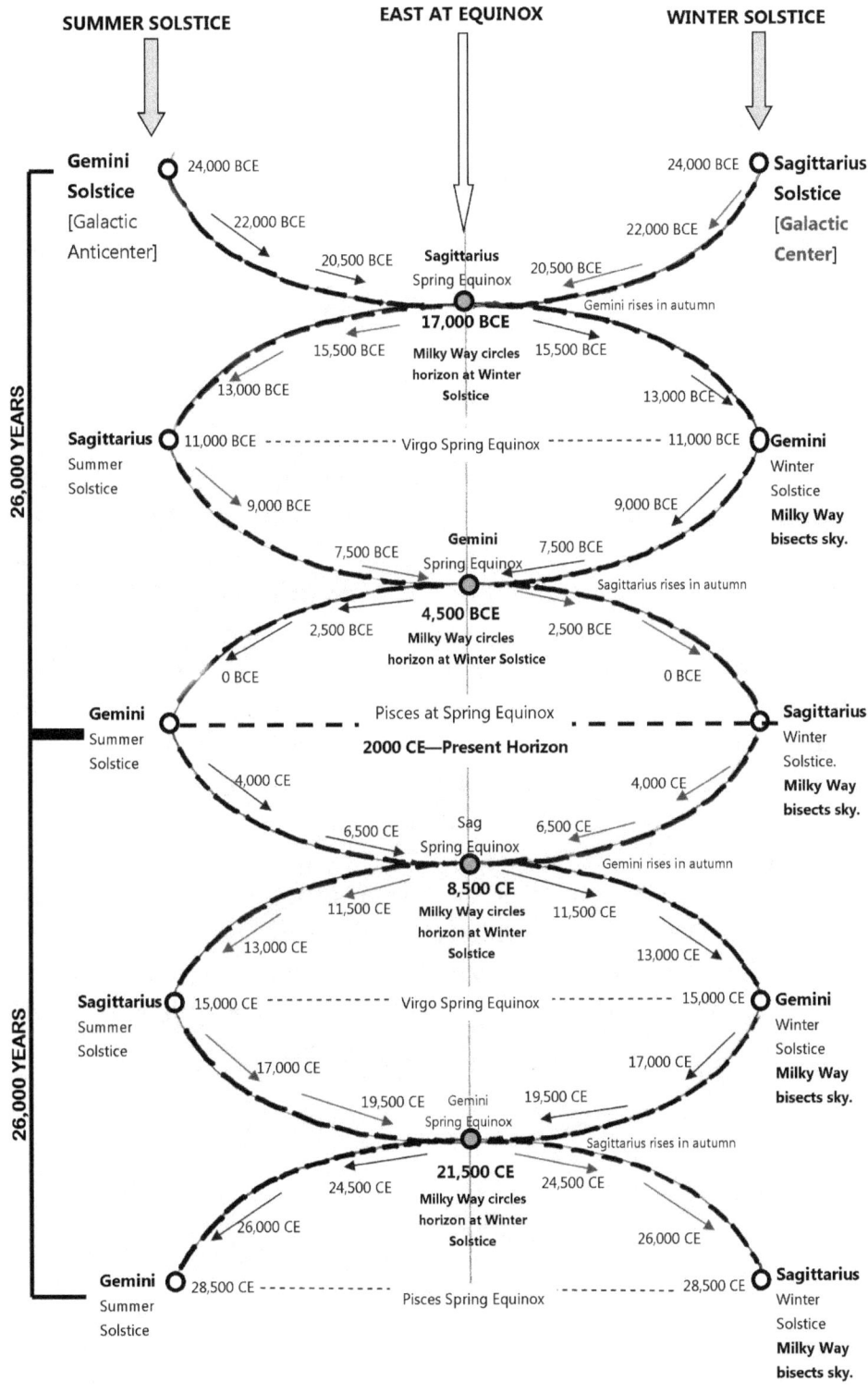

The Twirling Milky Way 24,000 BCE to 28,500 CE (EH)

Hindu astrologers call this period the Kali Yuga, the Iron Age, or Age of Destruction. The Mula nakshatra is linked to Kali, as its shakti (goddess) is Nirriti, an avatar of Kali. Mula means "root" or "foundation" and the central star of the mansion is epsilon Scorpio—a star at the base of the Scorpion's tail. Material life and souls are broken down, destroyed, and recycled in this lunar mansion. Mula spans from 0° to 13 degrees 20 minutes in sidereal Sagittarius, or from 23° Sagittarius to 3° Capricorn 20" in the tropical zodiac. The mansion encompasses Winter Solstice and the Capricorn Gate in tropical astrology. Mula is co-ruled by Ketu, the South Node.

Nirriti is a horrifying goddess. She is generally depicted as a malnourished, bony woman with a bush of untamed black hair wearing a necklace of human heads. She personifies death, decay and sorrow. Her name implies disorder, chaos, and lawlessness as well as the absence of cosmic or divine order. The term *nirṛti* is used to describe a place of absolute darkness and non-existence in Vedic texts. A trio of three rakshasas, supernatural beings with malevolent powers, are called the Nairrita: Mrityu (death), Bhaya (fear) and Mahabhaya (terror). The lunar mansion isn't entirely unfortunate for its natives. Natal placements in this nakshatra foster a desire for intense analysis, digging into the complexities of human nature and the natural world, and finding hidden truths. The search for knowledge may take the native into dangerous places and situations (See Syd Barret's sample chart on page 121).

The Western tropical zodiac is locked on the Sun's apparent motion and relationship to Earth, while the Vedic sidereal zodiac shifts slowly with the apparent motion of the stars. From the tropical standpoint, it will be centuries before the Mula nakshatra precesses away from that critical annual point in Earth's orbit.

Chapter 5
Metaphysical Mythology

Consider the Aeon and North Star shift lists noted in the previous chapter: the most recent ones were thousands of years ago, some beyond written history. So how do we know what happened? Ancient cultures left a legacy of evidence of Aeon and North Star shifts in the form of myths. Clues about the astronomical nature of these events are embedded in the story-telling devices.

Georgio de Santillana and Hertha von Dechend specified in **Hamlet's Mill** that the astronomical story-telling devices were elements that couldn't be removed from the narrative. Key words and phrases remained intact through hundreds and even thousands of years of narrative transmission. Plato and other early writers were aware of these narrative devices. It was a method for conveying wisdom that didn't require all listeners or even the story-tellers to understand the information embedded in the myth. For most people, these myths were just a good story. For the well-informed, astronomical myths were a valuable tool for conveying cosmic wisdom from generation to generation.

The authors of **Hamlet's Mill** encountered the chicken and egg problem: were myths developed to explain the shapes of the constellations and movements of the sky? Or did the movements of the sky prompt the development of myths and pantheons of gods? The answer seems to be persistent mutual influence.

Myth Categories and Story-telling Devices
There are different types of myths that provide astronomical information.

- **Cosmogenic myths** (cosmogonies) explain creation.
- **Cosmological myths** explain astronomical events, specifically aeon and north star shifts—critical celestial changes.
- **Theogonies** describes how gods were born or created and provides the genealogy of a divine pantheon.
- **Immortality myths** are instructive because they point to the means and paths for soul travel.
- **Astronomical myths** are based on notable star-planet transit events.

Consistent story-telling devices and plot features in multi-cultural myths were shared or derivative, exchanged through transmission over many centuries through many cultures. Even when myths have different characters and plot lines, the devices that convey structural aspects of the cosmos are consistently included.

Cosmogenic and cosmological myths explain:

- How the cosmos and the earth were made, whodunnit
- Who runs the show, determines the rules of life/death, sets the weights and measures
- Natural forces of sky and earth personified as immortal gods and goddesses
- The shape and parts of the cosmos and how these operate
- Life and death mysteries: how human souls were made, how souls travel, enter and exit
- What happens when Aeons or the North Star shifts

J. R. R. Tolkien's book, **The Silmarillion**,[1] contains the most significant cosmogony written during the contemporary era. Tolkien studied all the major cultural cosmogenic and cosmological myths and was aware of the many devices embedded in them. **The Silmarillion** sets forth the history of the first and second ages of Middle Earth. It properly follows the ancient traditional epic pattern and begins with *The Ainulindalë*, a creation story or cosmogony, and *The Valaquenta*, the birth of the gods, a theogony. These are a linguistic masterpieces, perhaps the most beautifully written of their kind. Tolkien came closer to producing a legitimate cosmogony than any other writer of the modern age. Sadly, it is flawed because Tolkien omitted or misapplied the key astronomical devices. It is much to his credit and evidence of superb scholarship that he identified and re-utilized so many of the cosmogenic devices.

Elements of Astro-Shift Myths

Mythic devices that represent elements of the cosmos may be characterized or depicted in different guises, but represent the same things:

- **The World Axis**, also known as the Tree of Life, the World Axis, and the Axis of Necessity. Other versions include the Egyptian djedd, the world mountain (Mount Meru), a grinding mill or manthana, a mortar and pestle, a spindle and spinning wheel, and a ship's mast. These mythic devices represent the

Babylonian World Tree

axis of earth's rotation that extends in both directions into the sky. There's a top, an axial shaft and a bottom. The bottom of the shaft is generally grounded on a structure that does double-duty as an entrance to the underworld. The top appears to wobble as the North Star changes, while the bottom remains stable.

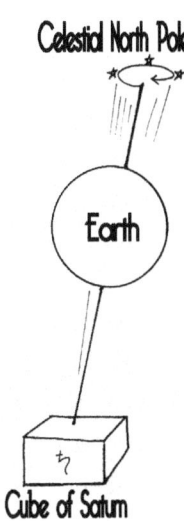

- **The Celestial North Pole** is the region at the top of the World Axis. It is the source of fate and destiny. In Egypt, it was occupied by Renenutet, the hippo-shaped version of Isis who determined a person's fate and destiny at birth. In the Greek version, it was occupied by Ananke (Necessity), Tyche (Fate), and the Moira, the three Fates that assigned each person their lot or portion. The constellation Draco the Dragon circles and guards the Celestial North Pole. Draco is assisted by two bears, Ursa Major and Ursa Minor. The Big Dipper is part of the Ursa Major constellation and was alternately known as the Plow or as a Wain (cart).

- **The North Star** may be called a Pin or Nail. In some myths a god or goddess sits on top of the axis to prevent it from wobbling. In Greek myth, Ananke occupies this spot and gives her name to the axis ("The Spindle of Necessity"). In Hindu myths, Vishnu or Buddha sits at the top of the axis, while in Norse myth, it is occupied by Odin's Wain. Arabic myth depicts Ursa Major as a funeral bier drawn by three sisters seeking revenge for their father's death.

- **Epic Churning Event:** Myths about time changes include maelstroms, whirlpools, a world flood, or a raging ocean. Ancient peoples associated the sky with water (the source of rain) and saw the sky as a kind of external ocean. The churning motion of the celestial waters, the Milky Way, constellational precession, and north star changes were disruptions in the relationship between Earth and the cosmos and described with these symbols in myth.

- **The Gap:** Heroes always have to pass through some kind of gap to traverse from the realm of men to the realms of the gods or the underworld. These gaps are usually dangerous and may include monsters. The gap may be depicted as an ocean, a mountain range, or a forbidding forest.

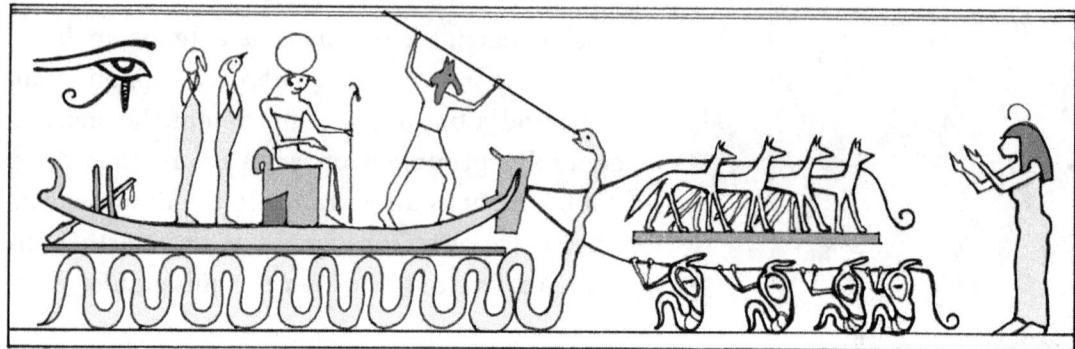

- **Ship**: the means for traveling into the underworld, the sky beneath the earth. The Egyptian Ra's solar boat sails through the waters of the sky. Odysseus and his crew also used a ship, the Argo. Other heroes and gods used a wagon or cart, a special animal like Pegasus, Odin's horse Sleipnir, or Vishnu's bird-mount Garuda.

- **Cauldron**: cauldrons represent the womb of the cosmos. They symbolize gestation and creation, stirring possibilities, and magical potentialities. Mythic cauldrons are associated with creation goddesses, legendary witches, and sorceresses along a spectrum of good-and-bad-assness. Some heroes are boiled to death in cauldrons, a metaphor for reincarnation. Cauldrons can act as a repository for the story-telling equivalent of cosmic goo. They are typically three-legged or boil above a fire on a three-legged stand, an item associated with prophecy.

- **Two or more cosmic realms** that usually refer to the sky above and the sky below. This is the Lake of the Sky and Lake of Duat in Egyptian lore, or the Mesopotamian underworld and the starry realm of gods. The Norse World Tree Yggdrasil has nine worlds arranged along the tree's trunk, with the Aesir at the top and Hel's realm at the bottom. The human realm is roughly in the middle, hence the term "Middle Earth." Myths aren't very clear about these locations. The boundary between terrestrial and celestial geography can be fuzzy. The tip-off is usually the extreme efforts and perils faced by those who traverse from one realm to another. Marcus Minucius Felix wrote that when Pluto abducted Proserpine (Persephone), she was carried "through thick woods and over a length of sea, was brought by Pluto into a cavern, the residence of departed spirits, over whom she afterward ruled with absolute sway."[2]

- **Bridge of Light**: in Norse myth, the rainbow bridge Bifrost, guarded by

Heimdall, allows the gods to come to earth at will. Egyptian gods "walked the earth" when their star rose with the sun. Light bridges are a special means of passage that are usually only accessible to gods and angelic messengers.

- **Snakes, Serpents and Dragons** that encircle the world. These have many names but are a consistent device embedded into astro-myths. Snakes that are familiar to astrologers include the band of the ecliptic, the galactic equator, the northern constellation Draco, and the Nodes, the dragon's head and dragon's tail. Hydra and Cetus are constellations that depict monsters that have roles in astro-myths, but not in time-shift myths.

Baba Yaga is a very old mythic character. A Russian friend told me it is pronounced *Ba-ba-ya-GA*, but there may be regional variations. Noted archeologist and author Marija Gimbutas investigated Baba Yaga.[3] She posits that this legendary character is prehistoric because of her distinctive characteristics. The theories presented in **Hamlet's Mill** confirm these deductions. Baba Yaga flies around in a mortar and pestle, a symbol of the world axis. She has a house that walks on chicken's legs. This relates to pre-historic sculptures of bird goddesses, the idea of winged souls flying into the afterlife, and bird constellations—Cygnus (the Northern Cross) in particular. Baba Yaga is said to steal the souls of naughty children, a diminished version of her role as a psychopompos, a guide of souls into the afterlife.

Baba Yaga riding in her mortar and pestle. EH

It can take a long time for archeological theories to become widely accepted. Some scholars continue to scoff at Gimbutas's Old Europe theories. They also scoffed at Jean Auel's *Clan of the Cave Bear* [4] series, which described Paleolithic life in a fictional context. Further research and archeological findings over two decades substantiated many of Auel's descriptions. Gimbutas's theories may be vindicated in time. Be that as it may, Gimbutas's analysis of the Baba Yaga myth is consistent with the cosmological devices specified by de Santillana and von Dechend.

Ancient lore about the cosmos is hiding in plain sight. Baba Yaga is given as an example to reinforce the idea that a lot of these stories are familiar myths and fairy tales. If you know what you're looking for, the cosmic and astronomical devices are easy to spot.

North Star and Aeon Myths

The Hindu myth called *Amritamanthana* or *Samudra Manthana*, "the Churning of the Milky Ocean," is an epic astronomical cosmos shift and immortality myth. It includes all of the important parts set forth in the sumptuously opulent mythic style of India. This tale is in *Mahabarata* [5], which was compiled around 300—400 CE. The stories it contains are certainly much older. It is in Sanskrit and is the longest epic poem in the world, containing 200,000 verses and 1.8 million words.

The story begins with the Devas (gods) in pursuit of Amrita, the elixer of immortality. The Devas could not obtain it without help, so enlisted powerful demigods called Asuras to help them get it. In the story, Mount Mandana, or Mount Meru, serves as the World Axis. Vishnu sits on top of Mount Mandana, performing the role of the Nail or North Star. The Devas and Asuras tug and pull on either side of Prince Vasuki, a primeval Naga snake god who wraps himself around Mount Mandana. Vasuki symbolizes the galactic equator. As the two teams pull back and forth on the snake, Mount Mandana rotates from side to side and churns up the milky ocean, the Milky Way. Vishnu sends his turtle avatar Nurma to act as the base of the mountain to keep it from sinking, a symbol of the Cube of Saturn or the South Celestial Pole. New gods and goddesses, new symbols, weapons and devices, gemstones, and new sources of prosperity and destruction arise from the roiling waters. The by-products of this churning process are both good and bad.

A cloud of poison arose as the mountain churned. Shiva swallowed it to prevent the destruction of the world. Every year in late February or early March, Hindus

The Amritamanthana. EH

celebrate Maha Shivarati to commemorate this event and the marriage of Shiva and Parvati. It's a solemn all-night vigil focused on contemplation and overcoming darkness and ignorance.

Amritamanthana explains the apparent churning movement of the galaxy and the earthly side-effects of the changing aeons and North Star. The tug-of-war between the Devas and Asuras depict planets and stars moving in opposite directions to create this distinctive cosmic churning effect.

After Amrita was obtained, the Asuras and stole the elixer for themselves. Vishnu took the form of Mohini, a beautiful woman, and enchanted the Asuras into giving her the pot of Amrita. An Asura named Svarbhanu disguised himself as a Deva and drank some of the nectar. Surya and Chandra, the Sun and Moon, saw through his disguise and informed Mohini/Vishnu, who chopped off Svarbhanu's head. Since he had partaken of Amrita, the two halves survived. This is the origin of the Nodes, called Rahu and Ketu in Vedic astrology.

There are parallels to this story scattered through multi-cultural mythology, including a medieval legend about the Holy Grail being stolen by a trickster deity in an attempt to bring immortality to humankind, but fails. There are similarities to the *Hymiskviða* in the *Poetic Edda* [6], as the Jötun sea god Aegir offers to prepare beer for the gods after Thor and Tyr recover a giant cauldron.

The story of Amlethi's (i.e., Hamlet's) Mill is a northern European counterpart to *Amritamanthana*. This story is found in the *Gesta Danorum* [7] compiled by Saxo Grammaticus early in the 13th century. Hamlet's original name was Amleth or Amlethi. Amlethi's magical grinding mill and millstone are stolen and placed in a boat. The boat sails away into the Gap—the void between earth and the heavens—and is caught in a storm. The boat is sucked into a maelstrom, a swirling, churning phenomenon familiar to northern mariners. The mast breaks, symbolizing the World Tree detaching from the North Star. The mill sinks to the bottom of the sea and turns the sea to salt. Eventually a deal is made with the water gods to stop the mill's churning.

The *Skaldskaparmal* in Snorri Sturleson's Old Icelandic *Prose Edda* [8] contains the expression "Amlóða mólu" (Amlóði's quern-stone or millstone). This phrase is a kenning or metaphor for the sea grinding rocks into sand. In a greater sense, it's a metaphor for the churning of the cosmos grinding souls to dust and recycling

Odin Rides to Hell by G. Wl Conningwood, 1908

souls through the celestial pathways. Amlóði's name implies a fool or trickster. The Old Irish name Admlithi means "great-grinding", and the Irish-Scottish world *amhlair* denotes a dull, stupid person. De Santillana focuses on the grinding motion and the frequency with which that metaphor appears in multicultural myths and legends.

Northern European peoples viewed the North Star as Odin's Wain, a cart that pulled the earth along on its path. Odin's patronage includes a share of the dead, as he receives the souls of warriors into Valhalla. His eight-legged horse Sleipnir is a symbol of a corpse being carried by four men (eight legs). Yggdrasil, the World Tree, is constantly being gnawed at and imperiled by Nidhogg, a serpent wrapped around the bottom of the tree. This is the Nordic way of saying that the stability of Earth's relationship with the cosmos is always in danger. The axis can and does shift, forcing changes onto the structure of the worlds.

De Santillana and von Dechend cite other myths that describe the World Axis separating from the North Star. *Amritamanthana* and *Amlethi's Mill* offer the clearest examples of how the astronomical story-telling devices are used to describe the cosmos and cosmic events. Other myths include:

- **Marduk overcoming Tiamat:** Tiamat is a primeval snake-monster churning up waters. Marduk (the Mesopotamian Jupiter) chops up the monster and uses her body to form the earth, mountains, sea.

- **Zeus overcoming Typhon** is a re-working of the Marduk-Tiamat conflict.

- **Apollo slays the Python.** Here the Sun (Apollo) is compelled to destroy the writhing galactic snake. Light (the Sun) conducts a battle with Time, the churning galaxy/stars. He has to kill the writhing monster who is making things churn, causing the axis to detach from the old North Star.

- **The Tower of Babel:** the tower, a metaphor for the world tree, falls down. People are scattered and can no longer communicate. The continuity between past and future is shattered.

Vivian Robson wrote that the constellation Draco "represents the dragon that guarded the golden apples in the garden of the Hesperides. According to other accounts, however, it is either the dragon thrown by the giants at Minerva (Athena) in their war with the (Olympian) Gods, or the serpent Python slain by Apollo after the deluge."[9] Although his sources are unclear, Robson cites multiple dragon stories that are either North Star or Aeon shift myths. The connection to Athena is especially interesting, since she is associated with birds, specifically with owls, weaving and spindles.

Aeon Shift myths

Aeon shift myths are fairly consistent in the use of astronomical metaphors and are persistent throughout global mythology. These myths have striking similarities to one another, which suggests long-term verbal transmission and cultural exchanges. Variations were adjusted to reflect the favorite gods of each culture.

- **Gilgamesh's** fight with the Great Bull of Heaven describes the end of Age of Taurus.

- **The Gigantomancy or the battle between the Titans & Olympians** is an Aeon shift myth that relates the end of the age of Taurus and the beginning of the age of Aries. A new pantheon of gods overthrows older gods.

Northern myths bookend the reign of the Aesir, the Norse pantheon of gods, with two events. The first event describes the Aesir gaining power after a war with the Jotunn. The second event is the fall of the Aesir.

- **Sayings of Vafthrudnir**, a poem from the *Codex Regius*.[10] It describes the Aesir's battle to overcome the Jötunn or Ice Giants. After defeating the Jötunn, the war-faring Aesir do battle with and then merge with the Vanir, an older, more magical pantheon, through a mutual exchange of hostages. The Aesir's leader Odin takes Freya of the Vanir as his wife. Some of the Aesir, including Loki, take giantesses as spouses. This is highly unusual! In other cultural mythologies, the older pantheon is discarded after their defeat. Another unusual feature of Norse mythology is that the Aesir receive prophetic warnings that their reign will end. Their immortality has an expiration date. A few early threats are squashed, but they know in advance where the threats are coming from.

"Ragnarök. Fyrir miðju myndar er Óðinn að mæta Fenri og bak við hann Þór að ráðast á Miðgarðsorm"
Translation: Ragnarök, the last battle. Óðinn attacks Fenrir is in the center, while in the background Thor hammers Jörmundgandur. By Johannes Gehrts, 1888, Wiki Commons.

- **The Götterdämmerung:** The final conflict of the gods is called Ragnarok. It's a series of events and catastrophes that lead to the end of the reign of the Aesir, called the Götterdämmerung or "twilight of the gods". The Aesir are attacked and overcome by the horrifying offspring of Loki and his giantess wife Angrboða—Fenrir the wolf, Jörmungandr, a terrible snake wrapped around the earth, and their fearsome daughter Hella. Most of the Aesir are killed in the conflict, but so are the monsters. A new pantheon of Aesir are led by Baldur, a vegetation-sun god who is reborn after the war ends. The complete cycle of Norse mythology encompasses the beginning and ending of an Aeon.

These examples are not exhaustive. They're examples of aeon-shift myths that include the cosmological story-telling devices that are more familiar to Western readers. There are astro-shift myths from indigenous North and South American tribes, the Mayans and Aztecs, Australian aborigines, south Pacific tribes, African tribes, and variant tales from Asian cultures.

48 ❋ Chapter 5 Metaphysical Mythology

Immortality Myths

Humans are obsessed with the idea of immortality and have created epic quests that end with the hero achieving immortality. It's taken for granted that gods and deities are immortal although that isn't always the case. Gods die and are sometimes reborn in the same or altered form. The obvious example is the agricultural god-king Osiris. Osiris was murdered by Seth. When the pieces of his body were reassembled by Isis, Osiris became—not just a god-king of the dead—but a dead god. Osiris retained his name, but his appearance, domain and powers shifted dramatically.

Osiris with mummified body. Wiki Commons

The death of Osiris involves aspects of travel into the afterlife. Osiris' journey is the basis for the Egyptian version of reincarnation and rebirth, and the practice of mummification. Many Egyptian gods are depicted with animal heads and human bodies. Osiris is a notable exception, as he was portrayed with a human head. Prior to his death, images of Osiris depict him as a pharaoh. As the king of the afterlife, Osiris was still depicted with a human head but with a mummified body wrapped in linens.

One of the most famous immortality myths is Homer's epic tale, **The Odyssey**[11] (circa 700 BCE, but the date is uncertain). This fabulous adventure story relates Odysseus's lengthy voyage through terrestrial and celestial locations, including a visit to the realm of the dead to get advise from Tiresias, the dead prophet.

Hundreds of years later, the writer Virgil re-created a Roman/Latin version of **The Odyssey** called **The Aeneid**[12], which was published in 19 BCE. The hero Aeneas makes a similar journey into the underworld. Virgil had excep-

Gilgamesh as Master of Animals, grasping a lion in his left arm and snake in his right hand.
Assyrian palace relief (713–706 BC) from Dur-Sharrukin, now held in the Louvre (Wiki)

tional access to the imperial library and its collection of ancient texts, so his version of the journey to the underworld provides unique information that will be discussed in Chapter 6.

In one of the great epic tales from ancient Mesopotamia, **Gilgamesh**[13] makes a perilous journey to the underworld to find his lost friend Enkidu. The story originally appears in Sumerian texts from around 2000 BCE. The Sumerian tale was recycled and appears as an Akkadian-Babylonian epic, circa 1400 BCE. Tales of underworld journeys circulated throughout the ancient world, demonstrating human fascination with the mystery of death, curiosity about the possibilities of an afterlife and the nature of immortality.

The mythic Greek musician **Orpheus** of Thrace traveled into the underworld to attempt to rescue his lover, Eurydice. The story received different treatments by a series of ancient authors. It appears in Plato's **Symposium**[14] (385-370 BCE), in Virgil's **Georgics** (29 BCE), in Ovid's **Metamorphosis**[15] (8 CE), and in **Bibliotheca**[16] by Pseudo-Apollodorus (c 100 CE). Orpheus may be depicted as a hero trying to rescue his lost bride, or a coward who refuses to die for love and mocks the gods by his attempt to retrieve her from the underworld. After his death, Orpheus was immortalized. Apollo placed Orpheus's lyre into the sky as the constellation Lyra. The alpha star Vega is currently at 15° Capricorn.

Orpheus isn't the only underworld adventurer whose efforts were immortalized by being transfigured into constellations. The labors of the Greek hero Herakles (Hercules) include a journey into the underworld to capture the three-headed dog Cerberus. Hercules's death was caused by his second wife, who gave him a shirt soaked in poison. Zeus chose to make his semi-divine son immortal and offered him a place in Olympus. A later variation conflates the death of Chiron with the transfiguration of Hercules into the Olympic pantheon as a god.

The Roman writer Cicero claimed he knew of at least fifty regional versions of the Hercules legend. These variations were eventually collated into the epic adventures of a single hero. The labors of the Greek Herakles are astro-myths that relate the Sun's annual journey by depicting the origin of the twelve constellations. The creatures he defeated were placed into the sky by the sky gods Hera and Zeus. A remarkably ancient constellation called The Kneeler was later renamed Hercules. It occupies the Helice, the circle around north celestial pole, and symbolizes dedication and the quest for perfection and immortality. This is a clue that immortality is linked to the celestial north pole.

The Giant Hercules by Hendrik Goltzius, 1589. (Wiki Commons)

Robson writes of the northern constellation Hercules that "This constellation was put in heaven as a reminder of the labors of Hercules. According to another account, however, during the war between the Gods [Olympians] and Titans the former all ran to one side of the heavens, which would have fallen had not Atlas and Hercules supported it, and the latter was placed in the sky in commemoration of this service."[17] In this myth, Heracles is clearly associated with a tilting sky and the detachment of the axis from the north star.

Natal contacts to the stars of this constellation give "strength of character, tenacity and fixity of purpose, an ardent nature and dangerous passions."[17] Ptolemy associated the stars of Hercules with none other than Mercury, the god who gained more jobs and increasing prominence over time.

Herakles is a good example of how ancient myths evolved over several centuries. These stories changed! The earliest written myths included material from stories that were circulating in the Bronze Age and possibly even earlier. Herakles myths share similarities with the adventures of Gilgamesh. Storytellers carried tales about Herakles around the ancient world and modified their telling to their audiences. Herakles became Hercules as the story was later transformed and retold by the Romans.

The enduring popularity of the Hercules legends can be attributed in part to ribald comedic components. Hercules was a bit of a buffoon! The ancients had a rich sense of humor that was pithy, bawdy, and even slapstick. Hercules stories feature uproarious exaggerations, failures and flops from his lack of thinking before acting, and incidents where he triumphs in spite of stupidity. This character isn't a towering intellectual genius—quite the reverse. It's the ancient version of "what not to do and how not to do it." Ancient peoples were skilled at making practical life lessons fun to absorb. **Aesop's Fables**[18] are another example of this.

People tend to think of Greek mythology as a coherent and static collection of stories, but that's simply not the case. The names of some Greek gods aren't of Greek origin, but come from the period prior to Greek civilization. Some Greek myths are re-tellings of older stories from Mesopotamia. A useful reference work for sorting out different versions of these stories is **Greek Myths**[19] by Robert Graves. Graves collected and compared the existing versions of ancient myths. Evolving variations are presented side-by-side with carefully cited sources.

Gods change names, old gods get new jobs, and new gods gain popularity. Graves offers a unique insight into this process in his book. Another way to compare the massive transitions of the myths is to read early Greek myths written by Homer and Hesiod (circa 700 BCE), and then compare these to Ovid's Romanized versions in **Metamorphosis** (10 CE), published during the reign of Caesar Augustus.

To offer a more contemporary example, consider the marked evolution that has taken place in the myths about Batman (May 1939), Superman (April/June 1938), Wonder Woman (October 1941), and Spiderman (August 1962) in the decades since these characters first appeared in comic books. The names, personalities, and roles remain intact while settings and story lines are tweaked to appeal to new audiences. Ancient myths went through this process over hundreds of years.

Additional immortality tales include Odin's sacrifice of his eye to gain knowledge of the runes, the Volsung[20] and Niebelungen[21] **sagas**, and the Celtic story of Taliesin[22]. An unusual immortality story is that of Demeter, who walked the earth after the abduction of her daughter Persephone. The goddess disguised herself and took a job as a nurse to the young Demophon. Each night, the goddess said charms over the baby, rubbed him with ambrosia, and dipped him in fire. One night the boy's parents intruded as Demeter was performing the ritual. The goddess revealed herself in her true form, and explained that their interruption had prevented their son from becoming immortal. Only his name would remain, although it would be attached with honors. She required the boy's parents, Keleos and Metaniera, to build a temple as a peace-offering. This is the legendary origin story of the Eleusinian mysteries.

Myths offer different means for obtaining immortality. A god or goddess may confer immortality on a particular individual. A person may—through chance or opportunity—gain it by partaking of a divine elixir. Another means is by making a perilous journey into the underworld. Underworld journey myths are of interest here because they describe pathways and means of entering the afterlife, the realm of souls. These myths sometimes include descriptions the afterlife and features of the underworld. These features are a key part of the structure of the Greek cosmos.

Chapter 6
The Greek Cosmos

The peak of Greek civilization followed that of the Egyptians and Mesopotamians. The Greeks were great borrowers, and their myths and cosmic structure incorporates features from earlier civilizations. The Greek cosmos is described in myths, but more specific information is given in the books by Plato and other ancient philosophers. Much like the cosmic myths and immortality myths discussed in the previous chapter, the structure of the cosmos includes a range of symbols and metaphors the ancient Greeks used to explain concepts of the underworld, the afterlife, and soul travels.

The Cube of Saturn: The Greek's mechanical concept of the cosmos is distinct from the magical motion of the Egyptian cosmos. Kronos or Saturn was cast into the underworld after being defeated and chopped up by Zeus and his brothers.

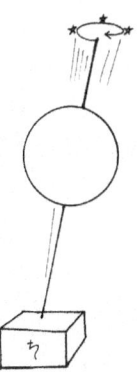

Located in the underworld or Tartarus, the Cube of Saturn acts as an unmoving base for the Axis of Necessity. It provides a stable platform for the axis. Saturn imposes the rules of time and duration, and the weights and measures of karma. Kronos (time) has the power to enforce death. The Cube is in the sky beneath the Earth.

Occupants of Erebus, the Underworld: Aídēs was the lord of the underworld, the first-born son of the Titans Cronus and Rhea (Time and Earth). He was known by many names, in part because of the fear and horror of death. Hades' names and epithets include Aidonos, Lord Dis or Dis Pater, and Ploútōn, a name later bestowed on Ceres' son by a mortal man. Ploútōn means 'wealthy' and conveys the implication that the riches of the earth come from the realm of the underworld. After the Titanomachy, a ten-year conflict that ended when the Olympians defeated the Titans, the three brothers Zeus, Poseidon and Hades drew lots for realms to rule. Hades won dominion of the invisible underworld, the souls of the dead and all things that lie beneath the surface of the earth. Astrologers should appreciate the importance of Lots in relation to Arabic Parts or the Hellenic Lots calculated for birth charts. Lots imply raw chance mixed with fate. Hermes and the Greek Moira were associated with Lots, and the practice of drawing lots was included as a factor in determining the path a reincarnated soul would take in life. Greek gods were subject to this form of chance and fate when it came to determining which realm the gods would rule.

Although he was viewed with dread, Greek myths do not portray Hades in a negative light. He was cold and stern but passive, and his role was to maintain balance. His subjects were equally accountable to the laws of the underworld. None were allowed to leave his domain, and some myths tell of his rage when someone attempted to steal souls from his realm. He was infuriated when people tried to cheat death. The rule of Aidonos/Hades was absolute.

Aidonos (Hades) and Persephone with Cerberus from "Myths of the Greeks and Romans". Drawing by Julie Hoffman, 1864

Aidonos was assisted in his rule by his queen-wife Persephone. Although she became his queen through dubious means, she got a good deal out of the marriage. Hades promised her "...you shall rule all that lives and moves and shall have the greatest rights among the deathless gods: those who defraud you and do not appease your power with offerings, reverently performing rites and paying fit gifts, shall be punished for evermore"[1]. As John Milton wrote in **Paradise Lost**, "Better to reign in Hell than serve in Heaven." The crown of Persephone is memorialized in the sky as the Corona Borealis, with stars in the early degrees of Scorpio.

The Greeks conceived of an administration for the afterlife—the Judges of the Dead. These were Minos, Rhadamanthus, and Aeacus. They created the laws governing the underworld and determined the fate of the departed soul by judging their actions in life. After judgment, souls were sent to one of three places: Elysium, the Asphodel Fields, or to Tartarus. The shades of the dead then drank of the waters of Lethe, the river of forgetfulness. Reincarnated souls aren't supposed to have any memories of past lives (although some do).

Other occupants of Erebus include the Furies, also known as the Erinyes — Tisiphone, Allekto, and Megaira. These vengeful hell-maidens live in a dank cave by the Styx. "Man's unholy designs incur your anger, rabid & arrogant, you howl over Necessity's dictates, and....by your power you bring the deep pains of retribution. Your realm is in Hades"[2]. The Furies were snake-haired, shape-shifting goddesses of fate, retribution and vengeance. They punished people who were guilty of hubris, those unholy designs mentioned above, as required by Ananke/Necessity. The Furies were born of Gaia after she was fertilized by blood-drops from the severed genitals of Ouranos (ie, the earth and sky). They are malevolent spirits who demand retribution for murder, especially murder of a family or clan member. The Furies were aroused by the ghosts of slain persons and could personify curses that called for revenge. Their earth-and-sky parentage implies that retribution for misdeeds is an implicit part of the cosmic order.

The **Eumenides** were the daughters of Hades and Persephone. Their job was to watch over lives of mortals. They had a role in dolling out the constraints of Necessity and punishing the unjust. Eumenides may have originally been a euphemistic, propitiatory name for the Erinyes. They are depicted in Sophocles' *Oedipus Colonnus*[3] and in Euripides' *Orestes*[4]. In late mythology, the Furies and Eumenides were separate groups of underworld deities.

Tri-form Hecate. Wiki Commons

Hecate was a Thessalonian goddess associated with witchcraft and sorcery. She was so powerful that the Bronze Age invaders and migrants from the East who brought Zeus into the Greece were too scared to tamper with her prerogatives. She retained all of her powers even after the new Olympian pantheon was integrated into Greek society. The dignities and powers granted to Hecate by Zeus in Hesiod's **Theogony**[5] (c 700 BCE) are quite impressive and extensive. She was a benefic goddess who gave willing aid to her devotees, and was of special help to herders and mariners. Through subsequent centuries, Hecate was very slowly and very carefully relocated to the underworld as a companion to Persephone. She is generally depicted as a three-form goddess. Hecate carries torches that relate to her role of guiding Demeter in her search for Persephone. Like Hermes, Hecate is a goddess of the crossroads.

During the Roman Empire, a horrifying underworld deity called Hecate-Brimo was used for the most malevolent destruction curses. Hecate-Brimo ate the souls of those damned to her. Hecate was one of the few goddesses that actually became more powerful between the Bronze Age and the Roman Empire periods.

Witchcraft was widely prevalent during the Empire period. Archeologists have found loads of lead curse tablets buried around excavation sites and many evoke Hecate. Her capacity for malevolence and association with witchcraft and curses increased after she was relocated to the underworld. In contemporary paganism, Hecate is considered the patron goddess of witches.

Panticle with symbol of Ekate-Brimo-Artemis. EH

Components of the Greek Cosmos

The Greek cosmos blended facets of the Earth and the apparent rotating sky. Locations and features are mentioned in myths and in some philosophical writings, but rarely discussed as a coherent conceptual cosmos.

Seven Rivers of Erebus (the Underworld): The seven rivers are the seven orbital paths of the planets along the ecliptic. Their paths originate from the Cube of Saturn. The planets must follow rules of time and space set by Saturn. They must follow their orbital patterns, provide time measurements, and perform their designated patterns of movement above and below visible space. Mars is river of fire and has the greatest scope for good & evil. (See image on page 57. Readers are asked to forgive the lack of spatial accuracy, as I was trying to cram a lot of celestial components into a single drawing. EH)

Eridanus: Eridanus is a southern constellation, a river of stars. The end of the river is the star Achernar (currently at 15° Pisces), a bright star near the south celestial pole. The mouth of Eridanus is called The Whirlpool, marked by the star Cursa (15° Gemini). Orion's left foot—Rigel at 17° Gemini—is in the whirlpool. The river descends toward Canopus (alpha Carina, 15° Cancer), a star in the constellation Argo, the celestial ship near the south celestial pole. Canopic jars used by the Egyptians to store significant internal organs during the mummification process are named for Canopus. All of these stars are associated with journeys to the afterlife.

The Milky Way is a band of stellar clouds that currently intersects the sky from Cancer to Capricorn on a pole-to-pole trajectory. It's also called the Path of the Dead, and is one of the possible roads that a soul may take to the afterlife.

The Metaphysical Cosmos ✳ 57

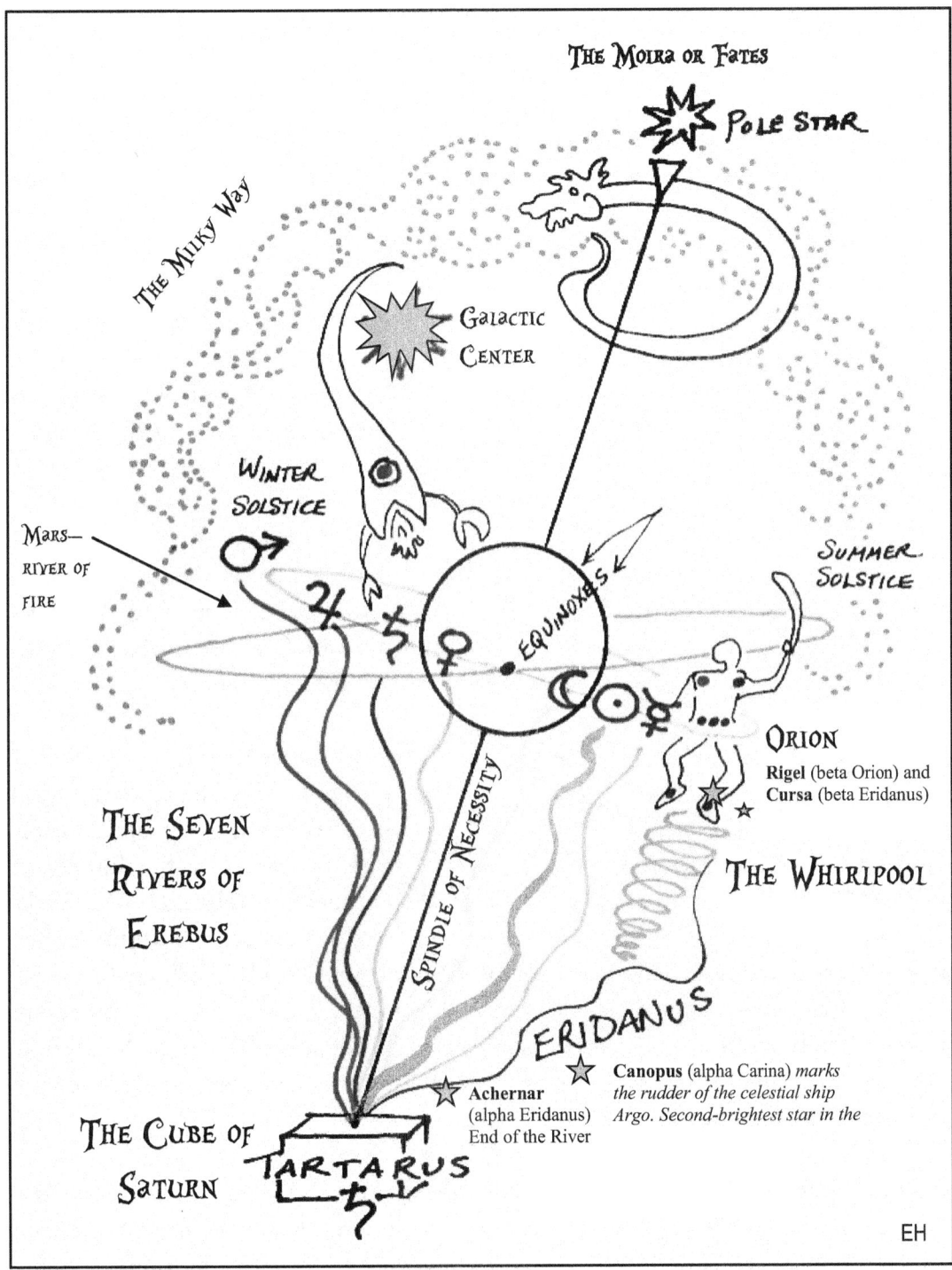

The Spindle of Necessity: The planets and stars churn back and forth around an apparent axis, the Axis/Spindle of Necessity, which grinds humans into dust and recycles souls. The metaphor of the grinding mill, the manthana, and a mortar & pestle are used repeatedly in cosmological myths. In the Greek version, the threads of life (human incarnations) are spun and cut by the Fates, who reside at the top of the spindle., the north celestial pole

Planetary Spheres and the Sphere of Stars: Earth is formed of elemental earth, which is surrounded by the other elements: water, air, and fire. Outside of the elemental spheres are the spheres of the seven visible planets. Each planet and its sphere is the domain of a planetary god whose unique characteristics and powers supply the planet's astrological meanings. Angel-like spirits or intelligences convey the planet's intentions to Earth.

Ptolemaic geocentric celestial spheres from Peter Apian's *Cosmographia*. Antwerp, 1539.

Beyond this is the sphere of the stars, which is remote but influential. The stars form a backdrop of location and meaning to the moving planets.

The zodiacal and non-zodiacal constellations relate to specific mythical characters and stories. The sky is a celestial library of characters and plot lines. Early Greek star lore is outlined in Hesiod's **Works & Days**[6]. This book was written around 700 BCE, about three- to four hundred years before astrology was developed. Hesiod gives mixed references, sometimes to specific stars, sometimes to constellations. The Mesopotamian zodiacal operating system hadn't been fully incorporated into Greek culture when the book was written.

Primum Mobile: the "first movement"; the workplace of the Cosmocrator, the creator of the universe. It is the outermost sphere. The void outside of this sphere contrasts eternity (stillness) with immortality (perpetual motion).

Physis (Nature): The Greeks conceived of Nature as a personified sum total of the creative powers or creative genius of the cosmos at work. All of the ancient philosophical schools had theories on its mode of operation.

The Platonic Cosmos

Plato was a student of Socrates active around 500 BCE. His writings draw on the teachings of Pythagoras, the earliest Greek philosopher, mystic, and mathematician. Plato's three metaphysical myths are **Timaeus**[7], **The Story of Er (Republic, Bk X**[8]**)**, and **Phaedrus**[9]. His books are usually written as dialogs between Socrates and other speakers, and they're very accessible to modern readers. Socrates had a wicked sense of humor so his dialogs aren't dry or boring.

The Story of Er is a highly detailed description of the journey into the afterlife. Newly deceased souls rise up along a golden rope into a processing center where they're judged and given penalties or rewards. Heroic souls are conducted to Elysium. These souls have the choice to return to human form if they wish, but are not required to reincarnate. At the other end of the field, souls are released from their period of punitive underworld incarceration or well-earned rest. Plato gives specific insights about a soul's next incarnation. Some aspects of a new life are chosen, lots are cast to determine random bits, and elements of fate are conferred. It's Plato's exposé of the inner-workings of fate and fortune assigned at birth.

Timaeus

Plato admits he's drawing on extremely ancient storytelling traditions in **Timaeus**. The title character Timaeus describes the nature and shape of the cosmos, the origin of souls, paths of life and death, and the rules of incarnation. He refers to a golden rope connecting Earth to the North Star, a device that replicates the Egyptian rope used by the Pharoah's ba-soul to ascend to the northern skies.

At the beginning of the book, Timaeus says that he's offering his "best story." It's not supposed to be a literal scientific description. Instead, the manner in which the story is told is the best way to explain complex cosmological structures with descriptions that are comprehensible to listeners.

Earth linked to the North Star with a golden rope.
EH

Here's the *Reader's Digest* version: The Cosmocrator or Demiurgos begins in a void. He makes two batches of cosmic goo. He uses the first batch to create the stars, then uses the second batch of cosmic goo to create the planets, sun, moon and earth. He arranges things in a particular way and then creates the elements.

Chapter 6 The Greek Cosmos

The Cosmocrater flinging cosmic goo to create the Cosmos. EH 2014

The Cosmocrator creates human souls with cosmic goo leftover from the first batch and disperses them throughout the cosmos, to the earth and Moon and "other instruments of time". He forges pathways for souls to move through cosmos so they can occupy bodies on earth, enact their fates, and return to an afterlife destination in the cosmos. Human souls are made of the same material as the stars. Souls are **star seeds** moving back-and-forth along cosmic pathways.

Stars, souls, and the pathways are intrinsic components of the cosmic structure.

When this is accomplished, the Cosmocrator sets the cosmos into motion. Planetary gods are tasked with forming human bodies that are infused with souls at birth. Souls is to enact the cosmic plan of the Cosmocrator as guided, empowered, and constrained by the planets and the Fates. Souls serve as witnesses to and participants in the Cosmocrator's creation. The planetary gods are in charge of setting and enforcing the weights and measures—the laws of Fate that steer the course of human souls. After setting the cosmos into motion, the Cosmocrator retreats into the utter stillness of eternity in the void beyond. Immortal stars and planets move in a design of perpetual motion.

Timaeus contains cosmic devices borrowed from much-earlier cosmological ponderings of the Egyptians: the golden rope, a soul joining a body at birth, fate conferred at birth, pathways for souls throughout the cosmos, and the notion that souls are made of the same substance as stars. The idea that the planetary gods formed human bodies may have a Mesopotamian origin. The Greek planetary gods enforce Fate on humans, but were also subject to it themselves. This diverges from the Egyptian belief that their gods were immune to Fate.

The Nature of Souls

In Greek lore, souls equal the number of stars. Souls made from the first batch of cosmic goo are called Ur souls. Some of the quotes provided below are from **The Aeneid**[10]. Virgil, more properly known as Publius Vergilius Maro (born October 15, 70 BCE in Cisalpine Gaul) was a brilliant Roman scholar who was extremely well-read and thoroughly acquainted with earlier myths and epics. Caesar Augustus commissioned Virgil to write **The Aeneid** (mentioned in Chapter 5). This book was supposed to validate the claim that the Julian family was the progeny of the goddess Venus. The hero Aeneas makes a voyage to the underworld. Virgil describes the journey:

> *"On they went dimly, beneath the lonely night amid the gloom,*
> *Through the empty halls of Dis and his unsubstantial realm,*
> *Even as under the grudging light of an inconstant moon lies a path in the forest."*

As a gentle reminder, Dis is an alternate name for Hades, and the forest is a forest of stars. Virgil continues with a description of **Elysium** as a *"serene land, where, in the world above, the full flood of Eridanus rolls amidst the Forest"* (of stars) where *"those hovering souls, people and tribes unnumbered"* move to the *"true Earth in Heaven"* and wait to be reborn.

Virgil mirrored Odysseus's underworld journey to consult with Tiresias in the episode where Aeneus makes an underworld journey to get advice from his father Anchises. The most important soul-related information Anchises provides is in this statement:

"Fiery is the vigor and divine the source of those life seeds, so far as harmful bodies clog them not" but when they have lived and died *"it must needs be that many a taint, long linked in growth, should in wondrous use become deeply ingrained. Therefore, they are schooled with penalties: for some – the stain of guilt is washed away under swirling*

floods or burned out in fire. Each of us suffers his own spirit."[11] Greek afterlife punishments were personalized to fit infractions, and Virgil preserves that tradition.

Virgil's passages are consistent with the Greco-Egyptian idea that souls are made of a fiery substance that is pure and divine. He explains that souls can become tainted or marked during a lifetime in a body, the equivalent of the Hindu idea of karmic stains. These marks are the cause of penalties in the afterlife, where the "stain of guilt" is subject to elemental cleansings with water and fire.

Virgil (19 BCE—19 BCE)

One might reflect on this quote in context with the Biblical "mark of Cain." Cain murdered his brother and was marked for it. Talmudic commentaries say that the descendants of Cain traveled far and wide, and that the mark was a signal to others that they were to be left alone and unharmed. Eventually, Cain's descendants traveled to the Moon. Ancient multi-cultural primary resources repeatedly state that souls occupy planets and stars. The **Bhagavad Gita**[12] specifies that souls may ascend between lives, planet by planet, as each planetary lesson is learned.

The 6th century BCE pre-Socratic philosopher Heraklitos wrote: "*the way up and the way down are one and the same.*"[13] This indicates that the path of souls is both an exit and entrance—all becoming is circular. Plato's golden rope takes souls "up" to the post-life processing center, while the path to Erebus is clearly "down," both underground and in the sky beneath the earth. As previously noted, directions to the afterlife are often fuzzy and contradictory. Writers use the prepositions "up" or "down", but what they apparently mean is "out into the sky." Souls need wings to fly through the portals to find the paths of dead that go into outer space, the spheres of the planets and stars.

Nine centuries later, Plotinus, a 3rd century CE neo-Platonic/Pythagorean philosopher, wrote "*The soul will therefore move around the center, that is, around the principle from which she proceeds; and, tending toward it, she will attach herself to it, as indeed all souls should do.*"[14] Plotinus has a slightly different take on the idea of soul-planet associations. He implies that each soul is attuned to a specific principle, the themes and lessons associated with a planet or star. Through multiple lifetimes, the soul will repeat the themes of the planet or star.[14]

In Talmudic writings, it is stated that: "*In Adam were contained the 600,000 souls of Israel, like so many threads twisted together in the wick of a candle.*"[15] Adam was the Ur soul, the original primordial soul on Earth. Many cultural mythologies, including the Old Testament of the Bible, feature humans that lived for hundreds of years. After the first, lengthy incarnation, Ur souls split into many other souls over time through some kind of cosmic recycling and development process. It also suggests that many souls are twined together in time-space. Edgar Cayce's writings on reincarnation[16] reiterate the concept of entwined groups of souls.

The Bhagavad Gita[17] is the primary Hindu text on reincarnation. In this book, the warrior Arjuna has an in-depth discussion about the movement of souls with Krishna before a battle. Greek and Hindu reincarnation concepts have some similarities and differences. Both Greek and Hindu primary reference texts indicate that evil-doers are reborn as lower life forms as a punishment. Plato goes so far as to say that the worst humans will be reborn as fish because they don't deserve to breathe the air!

Both traditions offer the possibility of escaping the obligation of transmigration by living a pure life. The Greek version specifies the attainment of wisdom—an intellectual goal. The Hindu version specifies enlightenment—a spiritual attainment. Is there a difference between wisdom and enlightenment? In the case of soul evolution, perhaps not. The use of different terms demonstrates different cultural priorities.

Fate, Fortune, Providence, and Destiny
Mortals are subject to these forces from birth. Although these terms are sometimes used interchangeably, they are quite different.[17]

Fate is conferred at birth. A person's fate is what the individual will experience regardless of all else. There's no choice about fate, but there is a choice of how the person responds to it (free will). In various myths, the three Fates are inaccessible to humans. Not even the gods can intercede with the Fates, and are subject to fate themselves. Fate is often linked to Ananke or Necessity. An event takes place that compels a person to act or respond out of necessity. As a cosmic force, Fate is neither good nor bad, but an individual's experience of it may evoke strong feelings one way or the other. Sometimes what seems like an unfortunate fate may be the very thing that compels a person to strive and become great.

Fortune is an innate quality, although ferociously determined people can make their own luck. People who seem more fortunate than others are thought to be favored by the gods and are called Fortune's Favorites. The goddess Fortuna or Fortuna Primogenia (the first-born of Zeus) is depicted with a blind-fold and holds a revolving wheel. Fortuna is blind and that the workings of fortune are random. Fortune has very little to do with meritorious deeds. It is gained by chance at the spin of the wheel. Fortune that is gained can also be lost. Fortuna's revolving wheel carries some to the top and others to the bottom.

Another view is that Fortune arrives when "preparedness meets opportunity." Perhaps those who are lucky are better at spotting and taking advantage of opportunities. These principles are embedded in the tarot's Wheel of Fortune card, which is attributed to Jupiter in the Golden Dawn attribution system. Saturn is the planet that rules time. The planet Jupiter's relationship to luck is through timing; that is, by being in the right set of circumstances at the right time to take advantage of it. On rare occasions, Jupiter is so beneficially placed in the natal chart that it signifies the good fortune of being born into a wealthy family or possessing talents that attract wealth with some degree of ease. Many astrological texts claim that Jupiter is a "lucky planet" but for many, that simply isn't the case.

Atu X: Wheel of Fortune. **Tarot Pink** 2015. EH

Providence arrives through quirks in the environment, through natural forces of weather, land, and circumstantial events that block or hasten a person's progress. It is often referred to as "divine providence" as the gods get the credit for interceding through the forces they control to help or harm the individual. Because these tend to be earthly forces, Providence is rarely recognized until after the fact. Providence is not a human choice, although prayers that appeal for help from the gods may be answered through Providence. Sailors lost at sea are aided by Providence if the tides carry their lifeboat to land. Providence may be evoked through a desperate plea that's spoken or written and cast to the winds, and results in some form of much-needed assistance. When a city catches fire, Providence is a wind that blows the flames away from undamaged buildings or rain that quenches the fires. Providence is at work when a person is compelled to leave early and so arrives moments before a critical event. The reverse is equally providential if a person is delayed from leaving for an appointment or journey, and then is saved from serious injury or death. For example, a handful of people were prevented from getting onboard the Titanic before its fatal voyage. Providence operates outside of human control.

Birth charts give clues to a person's fate, fortune, and potential for providential benefits or challenges. Planets in accidental dignity—a side-effect of the time of birth—are a type of fate. Accidental dignity occurs when a planet occupies an angular house*, a side-effect of the time of birth. The absence of accidental dignity is similarly fateful. A planet in a particular sign is a type of fate as the planet is attuned to that sign's range of meanings and potentials. Planets retain the nature of their condition at birth until the person consciously engages with that energy and transforms it to the extent of their abilities to do so. The fateful nature of a natal planet in detriment or fall (difficult dignities) may improve with age.

The rulers and occupants of the fifth house of Good Fortune and eleventh house of Good Spirits are fortune indicators. For example, a good aspect between the ruler of the first house and the fifth house shows the potential for good fortune. A good aspect between the rulers of the fifth and eleventh houses is a sign that the individual's guiding spirit nudges the person to take advantage of timely opportunities. The rulers of the sixth (Bad Fortune) and twelfth (Bad Spirit) houses are potential misfortune indicators. An aspect between the rulers of the eleventh and twelfth houses may indicate that a person can spot opportunities but is prevented from taking advantage of them. Examine the relationships between the planets that rule these four houses to get an idea of how a person may enact and experience fate-related situations. Transiting contacts to those house rulers will show when fateful events are most likely to occur.

A person's proclivity for experiencing providential circumstances may be shown by the rulers or occupants of the third and ninth houses, the houses of the Goddess and the God, respectively. Providence unfolds through events and timing within the daily environment, a third house matter. Good aspects to the ruler of

---

* The angular houses are the 1st, 4th, 7th, and 10th houses. Placement in an angular house makes planets strong and prominent, but it doesn't make them "good" or "fortunate." That depends on the nature of the planet, the sign it occupies, and the aspects it exchanges with other planets.

the ninth house show a person's prayers may gain divine intercession in the form of Providence. Difficult aspects show struggles with bad timing. Contradictory placements like a badly-placed third house ruler and a well-placed ninth house ruler may show that what seems like bad timing in the short-run may actually be for the best in the long-run. A third house ruler disposited by a malefic ninth house ruler implies that the person may do the right thing at the right time, yet gain no benefits from it. Oppositions between the third and ninth house may have a similar effect.

Destiny is the net outcome of an individual's experiences with Fate, Fortune, and Providence. Destiny is not one of the deities at the top of the Axis of Necessity; it's an earthly, human-made phenomenon. It is sculpted in space-time as a person moves through life events and responds with free will. People can "make" or pursue destiny by being ambitious and determined. Destiny isn't passive—it is a by-product of individual choices. Results are not guaranteed, though, as these can hinge on the vagaries of Fate, Fortune, and Providence. A person can forge a great destiny by overcoming the tests of Fate and Necessity, and conquering the obstacles that they present. The individual's skills, desires, and ambitions to attain some achievement are elements of destiny in that they are critical features of a person's character harnessed with personal will.

Character molds and shapes destiny. The quote "character is destiny" is attributed to the Greek philosopher Heraclitus, who lived around 500 B.C. Heraclitus believed that a person's character shapes their outer life and destiny, thus rejecting the idea of lives being totally predetermined by an outside force. Some individuals are capable of directing their desires with single-minded focus. A powerful Ascendant ruler has a role to play in strength of character, as does a well-placed natal Sun. Favorable chart placements include good aspects from helpful planets, placement in the house of joy, in rulership or exaltation, or accidental dignity. The Sun and/or Ascendant ruler as a rising planet is especially propitious providing it is not unduly harmed by a malefic, harmful planet.

Destiny isn't always tidy and clean-cut. Aleister Crowley might have fulfilled his destiny to be the greatest magician of the 20th century, but he was also a drug addict and a money-moocher. He treated others badly and violated behavioral boundaries. Audie Murphy achieved amazing military feats during World War 2, but after returning home he experienced a range of personal problems from post-traumatic stress disorders. (See Chapter 11, pg 131) It's the nature of human culture to deem a specific person "the greatest" at something, but that greatness may be specific to one compartment of a person's life, or may represent only a few years of an entire life.

Achieving a great destiny is not mutually exclusive with being a good person! It is useful to separate the acts or achievements from the person's lifestyle; or the person's lifestyle from the achievements. A person may fulfill a particular role in society that is fated or fateful, but in summation the destiny that is achieved may not be, in common terms, a complete success. Immortality comes with caveats in the fine print. Achieving great ambitions is not the only measure of success. A life filled with love, kindness, good relationships and personal contentment is a highly desirable destiny with different challenges.

The definition of destiny is a sticky issue. The more one attempts to sort out what it is or isn't, the deeper the quagmire gets. It depends on the yardstick that is used to measure and assess it. The most commonly cited yardsticks tend to conform to cultural conditioning, gender roles, and expectations promulgated by religious dogma. The ancient yardstick of spiritual evolution is the attainment of wisdom and/or enlightenment, but the 21st century yardstick revolves around the fulfillment of personal ambitions and monetary success. For some, the yardstick focuses on finding and keeping a life partner. The requirements for attaining spiritual evolution and freedom from the wheel of incarnation are contradictory to the contemporary requirements for a most contemporary life goals.

The sinking of the Titanic is an example of how the principles of fate, fortune, providence and destiny operate.

Fate: to choose to travel from the British Isles to the United States at that particular time; to be on board and experience the incident (cruel but impersonal).

Fortune: Some had the good fortune to get into a lifeboat before it sank. Others had the bad fortune to be left behind or be locked in the lower decks. The lifeboats were not entirely filled, so many more could have been saved. The bad decisions of a few caused bad fortune to all but the passengers who survived.

Providence: The iceberg in the path of the ship was a force of nature, a random natural element. Prior to the ship's sailing, some ticket-holders were prevented from getting on board by providential circumstances that were initially seen as misfortunes. There are records of several individuals who, for one reason or another, were prevented from boarding the Titanic. The stories of these thwarted passengers reveal a combination of fortune and providence.

Destiny: The sinking of the Titanic was due to a combination of human hubris, ignored warnings, inattention and bad visibility which led to the collision with the iceberg. The captain and builder were so confident of the ship's impregnability that they failed to guard against an obvious danger known to be present in the North Atlantic. The sinking of the Titanic may be regarded as Poseidon's punishment for the hubris of calling the Titanic "an unsinkable ship." It was a new ship making its first trans-Atlantic crossing, and never arrived at its first trans-Atlantic port of call.

The ship's name was particularly unfortunate, too. The Titanic was a twin ship to The Olympic. The Titans were the deadly enemies of the three Olympian brothers Zeus, Hades, and Poseidon. The lord of the oceanic realm struck back immediately – no Titans in these waters! Names are a component of fate and destiny, and only fools dismiss the enduring relevance of ancient mythic feuds.

Paradoxically, the epic nature of the tragedy guaranteed the immortality of the lost ship because of her perilous journey to the oceanic underworld! The story continues to tantalize public imagination a century after the Titanic sank. The rules for gaining immortality still apply.

The Fates
The churning movement of the cosmos creates sequences or waves of time where the past and the future call to each other, "the deep calling to the deep."[19] The cosmic fabric woven on the loom of time in the sky manifests through human life and events on Earth. This is one of the deepest mysteries of the cosmos, and it is at the heart of astrology, the tarot, and all forms of divination. People want to know what the weavings hold for them in the future.

The film **Wanted**[20] (starring James McAvoy and Angelina Jolie) centers on a fraternity of assassins operating out of a textile mill. Specialists read the threads in specially-woven fabric to determine their targets. The movie is a bit silly but the plot device is an extremely ancient cosmological metaphor for the three Fates.

The Three Fates by Giorgio Ghisi, 1559

Souls are a tapestry of individual threads spun by the three Fates, called the Moirai by the Greeks, or the Norns in Norse mythology. The Moirai share the top of the Spindle-Axis with Ananke (Necessity or Compulsion). The Fates are **Klotho**, who spins the threads, and **Lakhesis**, the apportioner of Lots, who measures the threads and weaves them together. The threads are cut by **Atropos**, she who cannot be turned.

Hesiod says the Fates are children of Themis by Zeus and sisters of the Horai (the three seasons). Sometimes their sister **Tyche** (Fortune) is included.

The Norns do the same tasks but reside at the roots of the World Tree near a well. The well was necessary because flax must be soaked to make it soft enough to spin into thread. Their names are Urða (that which was), Verðandi (that which is) and Skuld (that which is to become). Skuld relates to the old High German word *sceffarin*, female shapers who determine the shape of things to come. The decrees of the Norns were called *wyrdstufas*. The Old Saxon word *metodogiscapu* meant the "decree of fate" or "shaping of destiny."[21]

Three Norns Surround A Child
by Johannes Gehrts, 1889

Northern traditions offer unique nuances when it comes to ideas about fate and fortune. Wyrd is from the Old English word *weorðan*, which means "to come into being". It was a bad thing to be wyrdless and have no purpose, to never prosper and fail at every chance. The Old Norse word *hamr* indicated one's ability to control and shape images of events; *hamramr* means shape-shifting, and *hamingja* implies the ability to take advantage of good circumstances. *Ørlog* is an accumulation of past actions that influence the present. Those factors can come from anywhere, from family and personal deeds, from cultural history, and it is cumulative. It creates possibilities but also sets limits who what can be achieved.

These words from Old Norse, Old German, Old Saxon and Old English show an intensely keen interest in the workings of fate and fortune in those cultures.

Most of these words are either lost or have come to mean mundane things. A hammer is simply a tool, and weird just means strange or odd. Perhaps the spread of Christianity smothered Northern European ideas and traditions relating to fate and fortune. Word meanings change as they become more or less useful. Christian dogma attributes nearly everything to "God's will," so concepts of personal efforts relating to fate and fortune became less important. Still, it is annoying that a word as important as wyrd has been so thoroughly bastardized to the extent of simply meaning "strange".

The Threads of Life

Both the Greek Moira and the Scandinavian Norns are weavers who spin, weave, and cut the threads of life. Weaving was considered a form of magic and linked to a number of important goddesses. It was part of the Neolithic Package mentioned in earlier chapters. Making cloth requires many painstaking steps and skills. Cloth is an offshoot of agricultural development as threads are made either through the processing of plants or by collecting wool from sheep, goats, and other herding animals.

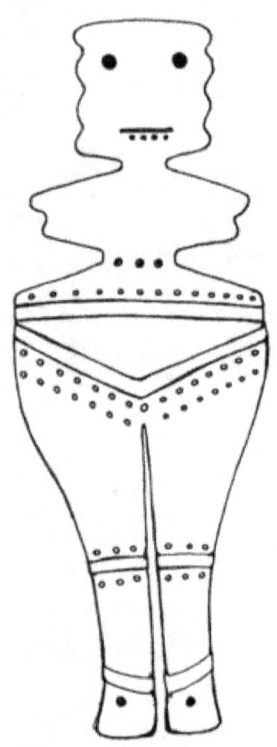

Spindle Goddess bone figurine. East Bulgaria, 45000-4000 BCE. EH

Flax is one of the earliest plants used for thread fibers and it takes a great deal of soaking and processing to turn into threads and weave those threads into linen. Having knowledge of all of those steps and processes was magical—a special type of magic that belonged to women and goddesses, much like metalworking was a type of magic that belonged to men and specific gods. A great deal of time and labor went into producing fabrics and it was an early source of wealth.

It didn't require a great intellectual stretch to correlate thread with souls as each life begins, develops, and is eventually cut off at its end. The allusion to weaving is equally obvious as peoples' lives are interwoven through family, marriages and other associations.

Marija Gimbutas found an ancient spindle goddess artifact in East Bulgaria that was made around 4,500 to 4,000 BCE. The Spindle of Necessity as a symbol of the World axis and preoccupation of the Fates with life-thread weaving is an incredibly persistent metaphor that's been in use for a very long time. The associations are simple but profound and enduring.

The goddess Pallas Athena is associated with this fate-weaving process. She is depicted with a spindle in some renderings, and as a bird goddess in others. Athena acts as a protective agent against the whims of fate and fortune. When Pallas Athena appears in myths, she provides characters with the knowledge and tools needed to overcome critical moments of fate so they may fulfill their destiny. In some stories, the tools and knowledge she provides change individual destinies, like the advice she gave to Perseus on the best way to kill Medusa. This particular story is enshrined in multiple northern constellations: Cassiopeia, Cepheus, Andromeda, Perseus and Pegasus.

In other myths, Pallas Athena's advise affects the outcomes of wars and impacts entire nations. She guides warriors who are in battles against an army under the protection of Ares/Mars. Recall that the River of Mars has the greatest potential for good or evil (page 56). The planet Mars orbits on the path of the ecliptic, while Pallas Athena is associated with the top of the Axis of Necessity or the North Star. When stories involving both Pallas Athena and Ares/Mars are viewed as astrological myths, they reveal a diametric contrast between the influences of the circumpolar stars and the planets circling the ecliptic—fate versus fortune, respectively.

Pallas Athena is called "the mind of Zeus" in late myths, but the spindle-fate goddess existed for thousands of years before the era of Homeric myths. This gives yet more evidence that concepts about the cosmos were known long before anyone had the tools to write about it.

It is useful for astrologers to think of the threads of life woven by the circumpolar Fates as a woven rope that passes through the Nodes. Each individual thread is entwined with the threads of people living concurrent lives. The Nodes appear as a one-dimensional axis on a chart. Re-conceptualizing the Nodes as a three-dimensional conduit, tunnel or tube transforms them into a portal through which souls and other influences (like karma) may travel.

Stars, souls, and the cosmic pathways are crucial features of the metaphysical cosmos.

Chapter 7
Mystery Cults and Soul Travel

Bronze Age pre-Greek ritual practices in Thrace and Thessaly were the progenitors of Roman Empire period mystery cults. The Orphic, Eleusinian, and Dionysian mystery cults spread and then flourished around the time of Rome's Severan dynasty, 180 to 250 CE. Mithraism was an offshoot of Egyptian solar-deity lore with similar goals and practices. Neo-Platonic Hermeticism was a subsequent eclectic blend of philosophy and spirituality. Cicero, a Roman contemporary of Julius Caesar, wrote "Much that is excellent and divine does Athens seem to me to have produced and added to our life, but nothing better than those Mysteries by which we are formed and molded from a rude and savage state of humanity; and, indeed, through the Mysteries we perceive the real principles of life, and learn not only to live happily, but to die with a fairer hope."[1]

The popularity of the mystery cults during the latter years of the Roman Empire period shows a trending preference for Eastern ideas from Greece and Asia Minor. Mystery cults focused on a god, goddess, or demi-god that died and was reborn each year. Rituals included symbolic re-enactments of the god's death, journey through the underworld, and rebirth. The focal deities combined elements of solar and vegetation gods. Dionysus was associated with grape vines, and while Demeter-Ceres and Adonis-Damuzi were associated with grains.[2]

Mystery cults offered in-depth preparation for the afterlife. Adherents went through intense initiations. Some mystery cults required initiates to experience a three-day incubation period either underground or in a cave. In an effort to prepare for posthumous soul travel, initiates had to memorize secret symbols and passwords.

Even after pagan religions were banned during the reign of Theodosius, Michael Psellos wrote[3] that the practices of the mystery traditions were never totally suppressed, and they persisted until the eighth century. Orphic and neo-Platonic Hermetic beliefs have had the most direct influence on Western occult traditions.

The Orphic Cosmos
Orpheus was a mortal who were elevated to Olympus after death. The cult of Orpheus began in Thrace as a reformed version of Dionysianism that was more ascetic, intellectual and speculative. Adherents were taught the secrets of con-

trolled soul movement. The central character, Orpheus, was a gifted singer and musician who (as previously discussed) descended to underworld to bring back his wife, Eurydike. He met a tragic death at hands of Thracian maenads who tore his body to pieces. The seven-strings of Orpheus' lyre symbolize the seven visible planets and the laws of sympathy and harmony at all levels of creation. After his death, Apollo placed his harp in the sky as the constellation Lyra. Other cult symbols were the tree and serpent, which should be familiar as metaphors for the Cosmic Axis and the Via Solis (ecliptic).

The Orphics constructed a revised version of the Platonic Cosmos. Different gods got different jobs and the theogony (genealogy of the gods) is altered. Kronos (Time), the father of gods and men, mated with Ananke (Necessity) to give birth to the primal elements, Ether, Chaos, and Erebos (Primeval Darkness). Kronos placed the primordial egg within Ether, and Phanes, the Creator, was born from it. Phanes and Night begat Gaia and Ouranos. Nyx (Night) remains supreme through reigns of Ouranos, Kronos and Zeus. Thanatos (Death) and Hypnos (Sleep) are the children of Night, but Lethe (Oblivion) was born of Eris (Strife).[4]

Kronos is called "begetter of time" and Ananke the "dreadful necessity [that] governs all." Ananke was also consort to the Demiourgos (Creator). This union produced Heimarmene (Fate). Adresteia, a Thracian-Phrygian mountain goddess, is an Orphic underworld figure identified with Ananke. The sphere of the visible universe was the circle of Necessity. The soul had to be prepared during one's lifetime to travel beyond it. "I have flown out of the sorrowful, weary wheel; I have pursued with eager feet to the circle desired."[5]

A surviving document of the Orphic cult is **The Orphic Hymns**.[6] It's a collection of propitiatory addresses and invocations to an eclectic mix of deities. The sacred poems were probably commissioned and written by a knowledgeable writer, perhaps a cult member, for use in rituals. The invocations are conjuring formulae that compel the deity to accede to one's wishes. Orphic prayers end with phrases like "grant a good end to a life of industry" or "grant a blameless end to a good life." They believed that good behavior and the proper rituals conferred rewards in the afterlife, or at least escape from punishment in the afterlife. A central belief was that the body was a prison for the soul, a precept shared by the Gnostics.

Astrology had spread throughout the ancient world by the time the Orphic cult became popularized. Astrological ideas were incorporated into **The Orphic Hymns**, showing their acceptance of the idea that the planets and stars had an impact on a person's fate in life. A passage in the Orphic Hymn *To The Stars* (7) states:

> O brilliant and fiery begetters of all.
> Fate, everyone's fate you reveal,
> and you determine the divine path for mortals
> as, wandering in midair, you gaze upon the seven luminous orbits.[7]

Orphic beliefs have persisted into more recent times. Amos Bronsen Alcott was a participant in the mid-19th century Transcendentalist movement. Alcott devoted years to a deep study of ancient texts and wrote a series of 100 titled aphorisms that offer a unique view into Orphic philosophy. The collection of his **Orphic Sayings**[8] appeared in the transcendentalist journal *The Dial* between 1840 and 1842. Although Ralph Waldo Emerson was one of Alcott's faithful admirers, the **Orphic Sayings** were considered folly and mocked at the time of publication. Alcott's work was a significant contribution to the revival of ancient mystical literature. Soul-related quotes from **Orphic Sayings** offer these sentiments:

> **Introduction** *(excerpt)*
> Thou art, my heart, a soul-flower, facing ever and following the motions of thy sun, opening thyself to her vivifying ray, and pleading thy affinity with the celestial orbs. Thou dost the livelong day dial on time thine own eternity.

> **3. Incarnation.**
> Nature is quick with spirit. In eternal systole and diastole, the living tides course gladly along, incarnating organ and vessel in their mystic flow. Let her pulsations for a moment pause on their errands, and creation's self ebbs instantly into chaos and invisibility again. The visible world is the extremest wave of that spiritual flood, whose flux is life, whose reflux death, efflux thought, and conflux light. Organization is the confine of incarnation,—body the atomy of God.

> **10. Apotheosis.**
> Every soul feels at times her own possibility of becoming a God; she cannot rest in the human, she aspires after the Godlike. This instinctive tendency is an authentic augury of its own fulfillment. Men shall become Gods. Every act of admiration, prayer, praise, worship, desire, hope, implies and predicts the future apotheosis of the soul.

Hermeticism

Neo-Platonic and neo-Pythagorean Hermeticism was the final syncretic religious offshoot of mystical philosophy and the mystery cults. It gained popularity during the third and fourth centuries CE, at the same time as Christianity. It was a VHS-versus-Betamax situation. For those who don't recall this battle in technological history, Betamax was the first commercially-viable videotape player, introduced in 1975. It featured a superior design but the units were expensive. VHS videotape players were introduced in 1977 and offered a simpler, less sophisticated and less expensive option. Consumers chose the less-sophisticated cheaper technology. Apparently the general public chooses its religions the same way.

Hermeticism incorporates elements from Thracian and Eleusinian mystery cults fused with a revival of Platonic and Pythagorean philosophy and cosmic lore, Egyptian star lore and magic, some Gnostic and Orphic ideas. The Hermetic pantheon includes a mix of deities from Greece and Asia Minor.

Hermes Trismegistus. EH

The central figure was Hermes Trismegistus. Hermes Trismegistus is not a dying god, but a psychopompos who leads souls into the afterlife. Hermeticism is a methodical spiritual discipline system designed to help the initiate's soul progress beyond the eighth sphere. It's the most sophisticated iteration of the ancient transmigration cults. Hermeticism was too deeply rooted in philosophy for the general public. It required adherents to be responsible for their own afterlives. It was anomalous because it lacked a dying god to provide a storyline for annual re-enactments and rituals. Hence the Betamax problem!

The key primary documents are a collection of writings known as the **Corpus Hermeticum.**[9] These follow the tradition of Plato by being written in dialog form, mostly between Hermes and his son or initiate Tat. Hermes explains concepts about life, the cosmos, the soul, and the movement of the soul between the realms. Some sections are easier to comprehend than others, suggesting multiple authors over several decades.

The Hermetic Cosmos is a further evolution of the Platonic model. The Demiurgos creates eternity, the cosmos, time, and generation. The cosmos is order, time is change, and generation is the life-growth-death cycle that takes place in time as governed by Necessity, Providence and Nature. The cosmos is beautiful but not inherently good; it is incomplete, always in the process of being created. It is said that reading the **Corpus Hermeticum** changes the reader even if the reader doesn't comprehend its contents. Repeated readings trigger deeper transformations. It is "the deep calling to the deep" in literary form.

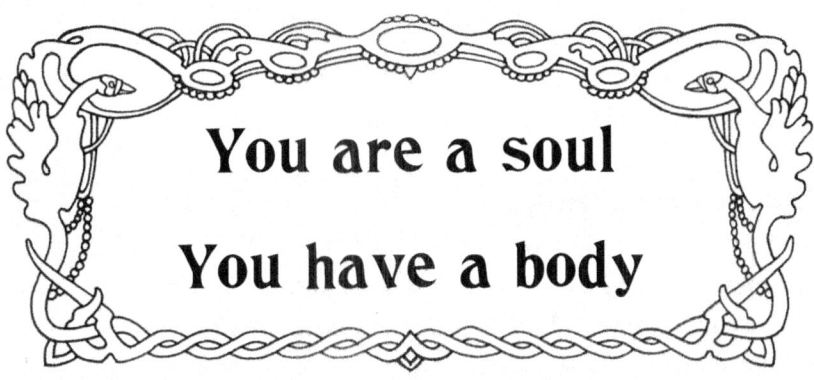

The Hermetic Soul

All creatures have souls, but only human souls have *nous*. Nous is the divine soul, a substance that permeates the entire cosmos. In Hermetic theory, human souls all come from one root soul, an Ur soul. In the spiritual realm, the identity of the soul is unchanging, but on earth, it occupies changing physical forms.

Humans are double beings, a mortal body and immortal spirit, souls clothed in flesh. The easiest way to remember this is: You *are* a soul, you *have* a body. The body goes from darkness to light as it exits the womb. The soul that enters body goes from light into darkness.

Souls are good, but may not remain good forever. They may become corrupted through Necessity experienced during earthly life. The soul enters a body because of Necessity, a quality closely associated with Saturn. In Aristotelian and Chaldean lore, the soul has three parts: *reasonable, unreasonable, and sensible*. The mortal body is subject to Fate as assigned by the planetary gods. The incarnated soul receives quantity, quality, good and evil—aspects of the material world. The **Corpus Hermeticum** gives a list of the virtues and vices that can be conferred at birth. These relate to zodiacal placements.

Hermetism promulgates the belief that knowledge of the soul can't be taught, but it could be remembered. When the body and soul are in harmony, the person gains understanding (*nous*).

Souls can be subject to the mortal body's tests of fate or rise above them. The option of free will exists, but it's incredibly difficult to avoid fate. Usually fate happens before the individual becomes fully aware that a fated situation is unfolding within his or her life. Fate is most visible in hindsight because its impactful, and causes (or creates the potential for) significant changes in the direction of a person's life path. Sometimes there is a choice. Sometimes the only choice is how one copes with a fateful event or situation.

The Hermetic Soul at Death
Death dissolves the union between the body and soul. The soul gives up the body, character, emotions, and desires—the unreasonable and sensible components of the soul. The reasonable soul re-assumes its natural substance of etheric fire and proceeds through the process of judgment. Attaining *gnosis*, *logos*, and *nous* in life helps the soul pass the Gatekeeper and enter the etheric realms. Evildoers are given to avenging spirits for punishment. Pious, pure souls become pure *nous*. Souls judged to be insufficiently pure remain in a restricted state for a period of time and are eventually recycled into another body.

The ultimate goal of initiates was to become Aion, the Hermetic equivalent of becoming *ahk* in the Ahket. If an adherent died with a pure soul, it would travel first through the airy regions where it would be purified by the action of the winds.[10] The wind gods winnow the soul, refining it until it is fit to continue on its way through the eight planetary spheres and stars. The soul surrenders and merges with God, reconnecting with its immortal essence. These spirits inhabit two places: planets or stars. According to Plutarch, the sojourn is shorter and less harrowing for souls that are less in need of purification.[11]

When the soul reaches the Lake of Memory, it must tell the guardians "I am a child of Earth and of the Starry Heavens. I am dried up from thirst and I perish; but give me quickly the cold water which flows from the Lake of Memory" or the Lake of Mnemosyne.[12]

The Metaphysical Cosmos ✳ 79

Phanes Cosmocrator or the "Modena Phanes" by EH, after a late 2nd century CE relief at the Modena Museum in Italy. The multi-layered symbolism suggests a synthesis of Orphic and Mithraic iconography. (see Godwin, pp 170-171)

Part II

Applied Astrology: Planets, Stars and Souls

Ohara Shoson
Five Egrets Descending in Snow
circa 1920

Chapter 8
Soul Portals

Creation myths specify that the Cosmocrator created soul portals that lead to pathways to and from the afterlife. These are an inseparable component of soul transmigration. No portals and pathways, no soul travel. The Egyptians saw the decans as portals. When a decan star rose with the Sun, it opened a portal for the star's deity to visit Earth. The decan rising at the time of birth provided crucial information about one's fate and soul journey. The Egyptian decan system is the most likely source of the ascendant and astrological houses.

Different soul portals were suggested by the Greeks and Romans. Heraclides of Pontus[1] (4th century BCE) wrote that there were three gates in the zodiac. A portal in Scorpio was used by Heracles at his deification; the other two aren't specified. Marcus Varro, a Roman writing in the 1st century BCE, also described three zodiacal portals: one in Scorpio, one between Cancer and Leo, and another between Aquarius and Pisces. These authors most likely referred to celestial locations between the stars of the zodiacal constellations rather than between the tropical sign cusps used in Western astrology.

Hermetic writers Porphyry and Macrobius[2,3] indicate that genesis and apogenesis took place through Solstitial Gates. New souls arrived for birth at Summer Solstice, and the souls of the dead exited at Winter Solstice. A further twist on that theory specifies that souls enter through the Cancer Gate, and also exit there if they are bound to return in human form. Only the gods and souls that are sufficiently evolved use the Capricorn Gate. Since not everyone is born at Summer Solstice, it's likely that the ancient authors imagined additional co-portals that allowed for the distribution of incarnating souls throughout a given year.

Four Major Soul Portals
There are various soul portals that can be examined in astrological practice:

- Solstitial Points—the Cancer and Capricorn Gates
- Eclipses and the Moon's Nodes
- Star Portals and Star Axes activated by visible planet alignments
- Generational Portals created by major planetary conjunctions

The solstices are consistently associated with soul transmigration; the equinoxes are not. The solstices accentuate the extremes of the Sun and Moon (longest day, longest night). Eclipses are dramatic Sun-Moon-Earth phenomena that change light. They are always entwined with the Moon's Nodes, points associated with karma. One of the most singularly fateful solstice-related charts is that of World War 2 hero Audie Murphy. (See page 131.)

Ideas about karma are primarily from ancient primary sources from India. Karma is a complex, multi-layered phenomenon that includes personal, family, community, global, past and future types of karma. Past lives aren't transferred in an orderly or sequential manner; bits and pieces of many different past episodes can be recombined in a single life path. In previous chapters, the soul's journey to the afterlife includes drinking from Lethe, the river of forgetfulness. The *unreasonable* and *sensible* components of the soul are stripped away so that only *nous*, the rational component, remains. The individual nous-soul merges with the River of Souls, retaining little, if any, identity separate from the collective river. There are many celestial rivers in the Platonic cosmos, all ending at the Cube of Saturn. Saturn is the Gatekeeper and the Lord of Karma, the outermost visible planet in the solar system.

A simple way to demonstrate this principle is with a glass that's half full of water. The water in the half-full glass is a single human soul. When the water from that glass is poured into a larger glass with water in it, the water from the single human soul is dispersed within the collected water of the full container, as shown in the graphic below.

A soul moving toward a new incarnation goes through several steps to regain individuality. Those steps are outlined in Plato's **Story of Ur**. Some qualities are assigned, some are drawn by lot, and others assigned by Fate.

A single human soul occupies the half-full glass.

The single soul joins the River of Souls and loses differentiation and individuality.

Planet-star alignments combine life path themes with planet-related traits and qualities. The star provides a general plot line that the person will experience, and the planet indicates how the individual is most likely to experience the story through choices, reactions, and responses. Bright combinations like triple planet conjunctions or double visible planet conjunctions with a Magnitude 1 fixed star tend to produce notable individuals.

Peoples' lives don't center on just one story line, however. Lives consist of overlapping stories and themes. Birth charts may feature multiple star-planet conjunctions. Sometimes the storylines are coherent and mostly harmonious, but sometimes natal planets and natal star-planet combinations can be at odds. Individuals face challenges when overlapping themes pull them in different directions. A major chart significator may lead toward something greatly desired while another important chart significator demands attention on something totally different. Consulting astrologers see clients when their various life factors are at odds, and this frequently shows up as slow-planet squares or oppositions to crucial natal placements.

Prominent Magnitude 1 star axes aren't overly abundant. An example is the double axis created by the Royal Watcher stars Aldebaran (9° Gemini) and Antares (9 Sagittarius), and by Fomalhaut (4° Pisces) and Regulus (0° Virgo). Natal planets must conjunct both stars in an opposition for the effect to be fully activated. Birth charts with the Royal Watcher stars on the major axis points ASC-DSC or MC-IC may also be notable, providing the time of birth is very accurate. Birth charts with strong contacts to the Royal Watchers indicate individuals who may face strong competition and life issues focused on handling powers and talents in appropriate ways. Star-related themes and storylines may be laden with fatedness that strains and tests the individual's free will. Fewer major star contacts are preferable to more star contacts.

Generational portals form at the degrees of conjunctions formed by slow-moving planets, and these include the invisible outer planets. The degrees of significant slow planet conjunctions may remain active power-points for many decades. For example, the lengthy Uranus-Neptune conjunction at 18°-19° Capricorn was in force from 1992 until 1994. People born under that conjunction will keep that degree active for decades. It was a sensitive spot in the zodiac before the Uranus-Neptune conjunction took place, and it is even more sensitive now. The axis at 18° Cancer-18° Capricorn relates to a cosmic—perhaps karmic—test of the individual's readiness to deal with fate. More specifically, this axis is associated with difficult family patterns and dysfunctions, a particularly troublesome type of fate that has the potential to impact an entire lifetime. Individuals with placements along that axis (The Gates of the Time Lord) are periodically faced with situations that they're not prepared for or equipped to deal with. The May 2000 millennial alignment in Taurus, which included a Jupiter-Saturn conjunction at 25° Taurus, also created a generational portal. The Uranus-Pluto conjunction in Virgo during 1964-65 was a portal that was made even more sensitive when it was opposed by Saturn in Pisces in 1965.

Humans enact bits and pieces of cosmological cycles as individuals and as collective groups. Natal planets attached to soul portals show what is significant in this respect. The collective side of the equation shouldn't be underestimated! A prime example involves people born under the 1952-53 Saturn-Neptune conjunction in Libra near Spica and Arcturus. From 1992 to 1994, members of this Saturn-Neptune natal group experienced a wide range of personal difficulties: marital break-ups, stressful care-taking for elderly parents, uncomfortable self-realizations, personal health issues, etc. They experienced these difficulties at the same time because their natal Saturn-Neptune conjunction was being activated by the transiting square from the Uranus-Neptune conjunction in Capricorn!

I called it a "group traffic accident" because so many clients had similar problems in synchronicity. Powerful generational portal birth signatures may also yield great benefits in synchronicity, but clients don't run *en masse* to get chart consultations when their lives are going well.

Comets are another potential consideration for soul portals. Mark Twain was born and died when Halley's Comet was in the sky. Classical sky-watchers associated comets with nasty natural phenomena and diseases, but being born while one is in the sky augurs a singular and unusual life. More astrological researchers are getting interested in this area of study. Perhaps they will find evidence of unique significance in the lives of people born during visits from comets.

Ancient traditions of comet-omens included determining the comet's direction, the constellations it passed through during its visible trajectory, the comet's color and the shape and color of its tail. The meanings of those factors remains somewhat mysterious as ancient writers weren't terribly forthcoming about the details. The omissions are strange because comet omens were taken quite seriously in multiple cultures and regarded as highly predictive. Comet omens were focused on affairs of state and conditions within society and only rarely had anything to do with individuals unless focused on the death of a ruler or the end of a ruling dynasty. The collective focus and sporadic appearances may be the reason that comets weren't integrated into early astrological practices.

Soul Themes

Energy patterns contained in the spiraling cosmos descend to Earth through souls that, through their incarnated lifetimes, perform intertwining and overlapping ribbons of thematic story lines and mythic story models. These are repeatedly re-enacted throughout the generations. This is why its useful to understand Egyptian time concepts: Neheh (linear) time and Djet time (overlapping vectors of cause and effect explained on pages 9—10).

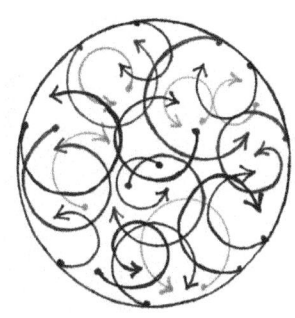

Non-Linear Time
Intersecting event spirals

Examples of themes and mythic story lines include the ever-popular boy-meets-girl trope. The outcomes of intimate relationships range from good to bad depending on the circumstances, actions and choices of those involved. Family relationships are another area of repeated themes. Parents may be excellent, burdened with problems, or absent. Children may be cast in particular roles within a family circle: the hyper-responsible oldest child, the peacemaker, or the black sheep. Life path patterns may follow certain trajectories that are popular subjects for stories and myths: a person starting with great disadvantages who makes good; a person starting with great advantages who squanders them; a person who climbs to the top of the ladder of society and business and then falls into ignominy; or a person who is ignored or mocked who devises an idea or invention that profoundly impacts the entire culture.

The possibilities are vast, but—with personal variations—these are story lines and mythic story arcs that are recycled endlessly by writers, poets, song-writers, artists, and other purveyors of popular culture. The boy-meets-girl scenario has been around as long as humanity and it still hasn't reached its expiration date.

One may note that genealogy grew quite popular as Uranus and Neptune transited Capricorn and Aquarius, both Saturn-ruled signs related to time and generations. Repetitive multi-generational family patterns will become more noticeable as family stories are reclaimed and more carefully documented. Pluto's transit of Capricorn coincided with organizations that track inherited DNA.

Apropo of Saturn-ruled signs, medical researchers discovered increasing evidence of hereditary diseases through DNA research, like the specific gene that gives the proclivity for breast cancer in women. Members of the generation born under the Uranus-Neptune transits in Capricorn could discover ways to cure some of these diseases through targeted gene therapy. Saturn shrinks and reduces, and strands of DNA are extremely small. It's strange that something so tiny can be so powerful and have such a profound effect. Technologies that entered into mass production during the 1990s, like computers and cell phones, have a marked tendency to get smaller, stronger, faster, and less expensive over time.

The grinding cosmic mill cycles and recycles etheric fire, the primal substance of both stars and souls.

Additional Soul Portals
Cancer Gate: last 10 degrees of Gemini, which includes
The North Star (currently Polaris): 28-29° Gemini
Capricorn Gate: last 10 degrees of Sagittarius, which includes
The Galactic Center: 26° Sagittarius. The goddess at the entrance to the afterlife is the many-breasted Scorpion Goddess called Selket-Serket (Egyptian) or Ishara-tam-tim (Babylonian), appropriate because the Galactic Center is nestled within the stars of the Scorpion's tail. The Galactic Anti-Center is at 26° Gemini, close to the star that marks the tip of the Bull's northern horn.

Rigel/The Whirlpool : 16° Gemini. This degree is the North Node of Venus and quite near the Node of Uranus; it was also the location for visible Venus-Sun conjunctions/occultations in 2004 and 2012. This degree is as sensitive as a shaved hedgehog.
Sirius (Sothis, or Sepdet-Isis): The Dog Star at 13° Cancer
Canopus (the Ship's rudder): 15° Cancer
The Ship of the Dead Dragon: 18-20° degrees of Taurus
Gate of the Kosmocrator: the last 10 degrees of Taurus, containing the stars of Perseus, including
Caput Algol: 26° Taurus, reputed to be an evil star. It's a binary star with bright and dim cycles

Toliman (alpha Centauri): 29° Scorpio (opposite the Kosmocrator's Gate and the Pleiades)
Sadalsu'ud and Deneb al Giedi: 23° Aquarius, stars in Aquarius and Capricorn
Gates of the Time Lord: 18-19° Capricorn/Cancer

Lunar and Planetary Nodes
Like the Moon's Nodes, planetary nodes are the degrees where a planet moves north and south on the ecliptic. Planetary north nodes form an axis with the south nodes at the opposite sign and degree. Unlike the Moon, which revolves around Earth, the planetary nodes are fixed points in the zodiac. The Sun is at the center and has no nodes; nodes require an orbit around a central celestial body.

Planetary North Nodes (South Nodes are at the opposite degree)

Mercury	18° Taurus 16'
Venus	16° Gemini 38'
Mars	19° Taurus 31'
Jupiter	10° Cancer 25'
Saturn	23° Cancer 36'
Uranus	14° Gemini 00'
Neptune	11° Leo 41'
Pluto	20° Cancer 13'

Few astrologers work with the planetary nodes, but they are worthy of consideration. Nodes are crossing points, so a planet that is conjunct or square it's own nodes is at a point of change. A planet conjunct its north node is about to move north in declination. This is generally considered to be positive. When a planet transits its south node, it heads south in declination. This is considered a weaker position in declination as a planet "hits bottom" at around 23° South.

This list of soul portals represents portal degrees and celestial features connected to soul travel mentioned in the research sources on this subject. Additional points may be worthy of consideration.

The Purpose of Soul Portals

What happens when a natal planet or chart point is conjunct a soul portal? What does it mean? A natal conjunction to a soul portal signifies fateful experiences that incorporate the meaning of that particular portal—a fixed star, an eclipse, solstice degree, etc.—that compel the individual to make choices that result in destiny. The interpretation of natal soul portal contacts may be explicated with the significations of the zodiac sign, house, and any aspects to that contact. A portal connection could manifest as a special talent, propensities for certain kinds of behavior, or attracting certain kinds of people. The portal could be favorable or challenging. What matters is what the individual chooses to do with the energies.

Past lives are not re-runs of a syndicated television series. Refer to the analogy of the soul as a half-glass of water being poured into a fuller glass that represents the River of Souls. A hodge-podge of elements from a myriad of past lives may manifest during an incarnation without any apparent rhyme or reason. Several bits of past-life karma may play out simultaneously. Talents from one past life could coincide with a spouse from a different incarnation, with parents, children or friends from another past life, and an illness or obstacle from yet another.

Some of the pieces and parts may not fit together very well! A clue to a person's comfort in life can be judged by examining the Ascendant and the Ascendant's ruling planet, which is considered the ruler of the chart. Determine if the Ascendant is conjunct a portal. Give first consideration to the traditional sign ruler and leave Uranus, Neptune and Pluto for later. A major Ptolemaic aspect from the chart ruler to the Ascendant, good or difficult, is better than no aspect at all. If the Ascendant ruler makes no major aspect (even by sign) to the Ascendant, it can't "see" the rising sign. As Project Hindsight translator Robert Schmidt phrased it, the pilot of the ship of life isn't steering the ship! Things will tend to happen willy-nilly and give the sense that the person doesn't have any control over what happens in life. The ship of life can get lost at sea, get stuck on a sandbank, capsize, end up in the wrong place, and a lot of other troublesome stuff.

An Ascendant benefits from planetary guidance. If the chart ruler makes no contact with the Ascendant, look for aspects from other planets to the Ascendant, particularly from the rulers of the signs occupied by the Sun or Moon, the stronger of which depends on a diurnal or nocturnal birth. These planets may perform the role of a first mate or co-pilot, and give some reassurance that a responsible planetary god is guiding the ship. The invisible outer planets give dubious aid in this respect. The Almuten or final dispositor are good potential candidates for this job, although not all charts have a final dispositor.

The Ascendant's ruler is supposed to be in charge of the ship of life, and this planet's relationship to the Ascendant says a great deal about the ease or difficulty with which a person encounters fate and fortune. If the captain is down in the head having a smoke, he isn't actively guiding the ship. Matters can run amok, and opportunities to advance in life will be missed or spoiled. An Ascendant ruler that squares or opposes the Ascendant by sign or degree indicates that the individual may have to fight against Fate or have brawls with Fortuna. A trine or sextile is highly preferable and is a type of favorable accidental dignity that makes the person's journey through life a great deal easier. providing other chart indicators support that conclusion.

Another indication of the soul's relative ease during an incarnation is the level of comfort or discomfort in the balance between the Sun, Moon, and Ascendant. Aspects to the Part of Spirit (the Lot of the Sun) and Part of Fortune (the Lot of the Moon) are a further clues of relative comfort in life.

The Ascendant, the Ascendant ruler, Sun, Moon, and the Lots of the Sun and Moon are fate indicators. If any of these points are conjunct a soul portal, the distinctive meaning of that portal is infused with the individual's life path. For example, if a person's Sun is conjunct the fixed star Rigel, that individual will participate somehow in the ambient cultural or the vortex of current trends by gathering and disseminating information and knowledge relevant to the times. Rigel gives riches and success along with mechanical and inventive abilities. However, it may augur perilous journeys, issues with knees or feet, and potential problems from the individual's eccentric appetites. Rigel's associated planets are Jupiter and Saturn, so the condition of those planets will give additional insights on how the soul portal's thematic narratives are expressed during the person's lifetime. The first chart in Chapter 11 (page 121) provides a powerful example of Rigel at work.

The house position of a natal planet-soul portal conjunction should be taken into consideration, along with the significations provided by characteristic attributes of the natal planet that's conjunct the portal and its relationship to the sign's ruler. If the soul portal is a star, examine the two planets attributed to that star. The combined portal-planet influences will manifest in the area of life shown by the house. These themes may also be carried out in the house(s) that the planet rules. Personality traits and activities from soul portals are most evident when they are *not* traits or propensities shared by or common to the family of origin. These traits, preferences, or abilities may be so anomalous that other family members consider the person freakishly odd. For instance, if a person has notable artistic abilities in a family where no known relatives have possessed that trait, an active soul portal may at work. Talent came to that individual from an unknown source, and an astrologer may find it connected to a soul portal.

There is no standard quantity for natal star and/or soul portal contacts. Some charts may have very few or none while other charts have multiple contacts. And there is no guarantee that a soul portal contact is inherently beneficial. Natal soul portal contacts are like accidental dignities; they show up in the birth chart as elements of fate, fortune, and karma cooties or karma cookies that are linked to the soul on its path to incarnation.

Avoid assigning qualitative values (good/bad) to soul portals. For example, a Sagittarius man with Jupiter conjunct Caput Algol carved a worthy destiny by becoming a welder and a lead guitarist in a death metal band. This might seem like a terrible placement for his Sun sign ruler, but he was able to do good things with it by embracing metal, both the substance and musical genre, and the darker aspects of mysticism. It is rarely mentioned that the Medusa's scales were made of metal. Familiarity with the details embedded in myths gives a grasp of the potential significations of stars.

Fixed Stars
Specific fixed stars are included in the list of star portals. These are magnitude 1 stars, the brightest and most significant stars in the sky. All stars have the potential for soul-portal significations; the relative importance of the natal contact determines the impact on the individual life.

For example, a person whose natal chart has a planet conjunct an unnamed magnitude 5 star in the sixth house with few aspects to other planets may not experience much in the way of influence from the contact. It may signify more about the person's work environment, co-workers, aunts and uncles, or small pets than it does about the overall life path or the possibility of health problems. Weighing planetary strengths and the impact of vital house rulers is at the core of chart interpretation.

Stars are embedded with thematic narratives, threads of stories and lore. They are connected with the afterlife and transmigration. The Egyptians, Mesopotamians, Greeks, and Hindus all believed that evolved and perfected souls occupy stars and planets. Recollect the words of Plotinus regarding the soul revolving around its center: *"around the principle from which she proceeds..."* A significant star-planet combination is a clue to the soul's central principle, its focal themes. Some souls are multi-taskers and must juggle two or more soul-portal themes.

Stars are associated with fated life elements. Author and satirist Terry Pratchett calls this **narrativium** or **narrative causality**[3]—the tendency for individuals to become the protagonist in the thread of a story that repeats again and again through human civilization. Stars and constellations are a repository for stories, a celestial library of human experience: the ever-revolving twins, the nurse-maid that raised Zeus, the wife who sacrifices herself for her family, the vain queen that strapped into a chair for her excessive pride, the lion defeated by Herakles, the libidinous hunter Orion and his painful demise, etc.

As you should be aware after reading Chapter 5 on aeon-shift and north star myths, a great deal of mythology is either related to or inspired by the planets and stars. Mythology is the basis of meaning for the planets and zodiac signs. Ancient astrology writers didn't need to include those stories *because everybody knew them*. It would have been a waste of space.

Stars "cast no light" so only conjunctions to planets and axis points are considered. The Egyptians attributed critical importance to the heliacal rising star. The heliacal rising star contributes significant emphasis because it's conjunct the Sun. The impact of stellar parans may mean that the heliacal rising star is not precisely conjunct the Sun's zodiacal degree, but it may be in contact with another natal planet. Or, for instance, a person born during the afternoon may have

the heliacal rising star at the Midheaven. If the heliacal rising star is doing double-duty in this kind of way, the star has a greater impact on central life themes.

It is valuable to determine the heliacal rising star on the day of birth and consider its potential influence on the Sun, along with its house placement at the hour of birth. Heliacal rising stars remain the same for several days, but not everyone is born at sunrise! Bernadette Brady's fixed star book[4] demonstrates how to calculate the heliacal star for the date and location of birth.

The orb used with stars is very small, usually one degree, perhaps two degrees for a Magnitude 1 star. Star magnitudes are rated in comparison to Sirius (alpha Canis Major), the brightest star in the sky. Magnitude 1 and 2 stars are very bright. If a natal planet is conjunct a first magnitude star, it indicates that the individual is prone to fateful plot-lines linked to that star. The theme or story lines attached to that star or its constellation *must* be enacted in life in a small or large way. Fate and karma aren't mutually exclusive. Stars are equally likely to show dharma, work that must be done in life.

Learning the locations of fixed stars takes time and effort; learning how to interpret them presents difficulties. Ancient and medieval star meanings can be vile; writers tended to state the worst-case scenario. A bad star like Caput Algol can have a good side; a good star like Spica can have a bad side. The characteristics of the planet contacting the star and the aspects to that planet-star conjunction have a significant role in how the stellar narrativium is expressed. Asking detailed questions of clients will help elucidate how star-planet contacts manifest. It's a mutual process of discovery and can often lead to surprises. The more an astrologer understands about planet and star meanings, the more easily relevant interpretations rise to the surface.

Ebertin's star book[5] is moderately useful for slightly updated star lore, but his star list is incomplete. Brady's star books are more comprehensive in relating constellational myths, but her modernized meanings aren't entirely convincing. Robson's star book[6] is the crusty classic since it's fairly complete and offers a range of antique meanings. In some cases, there's not much interpretive substance to work with. **Little Book of Fixed Stars** (2020)[7] provides a handy-reference list of 250 fixed stars with short meanings and 2020 star positions. **Secrets of the Ancient Skies**[8] is Diana K. Rosenberg's two-volume magnum opus on fixed stars. The information is comprehensive but not easily referenced. Books with information about the Arabic or Hindu lunar mansions give some sense of the meanings of star asterisms. Allen's book[9] on star names provides good summaries of the mythic narratives connected to stars and constellations. Since there are thousands of stars, its unlikely that any book about fixed stars will ever be complete. There are star lore books in Arabic that have never been translated, which is frustrating. The Egyptian decan lore is just now being revived, so it's hard to tell how much will be recovered or if it will be of use to astrologers.

It is difficult to predict at birth how star-portal contacts will manifest. It's easier when the person has become an adult and a cumulative picture of a person's life is available. Once a person begins to interact at a mature level in society, the star-charged thematic patterns become more clear and are easier to spot.

Chapter 9

The Moon's Nodes and Mercury

The Same and Different
Let's return very briefly to Plato's discussion of the two batches of cosmic goo in **Timaeus**. Stars were made with the first batch, and planets were made with the second batch. Why were there two batches? **Because stars move in one direction, and planets in another.** They appear to churn back and forth in the sky. Plato calls this "the same and different." What moves in the same direction as the stars?

The Moon's Nodes travel backwards through the zodiac, so in that sense they are distinctly star-like. In Hindu astrology, the Nodes are called Rahu and Ketu, and are the head and tail of an immortal Asura who is the enemy of the Sun and Moon. This means the Nodes are hostile towards the sources of life: free will, fertility, emotional intimacy, identity, individuality, selfhood, and self-determination. Hindu astrologers say that they spoil the houses they occupy. Rahu and Ketu put flies in the soup of life.

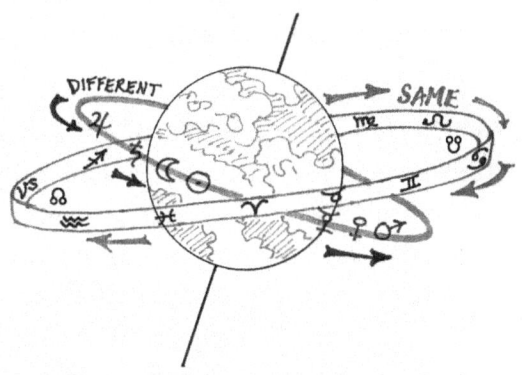

Rahu and Ketu are friends with Mercury, the planet that retrogrades most frequently. In the Western dignity system, the North Node exalts in Mercury's sign Gemini, a mutable sign where things are easily changed and adjusted. The South Node exalts in Sagittarius, a Jupiter-ruled mutable sign that's prone to excess.

Characteristics of the Moon's Nodes
- The Nodal axis is the third major axis (opposition) in an astrological chart, along with the ASC-DSC axis and the MC-IC axis.

- The Nodes move backwards, contrary to normal planetary motion, but consistent with stellar motion.

- The Nodes are *shadow planets*. They don't have bodies, so must operate through invisible, intangible, and symbolic means, creeping around in the shadows of our minds. Their operative modes may include metaphors, glyphs, omens, dreams, images, poetry, music, dance, art, visions, concepts, and abstract ideas.

- Although the Nodes don't have bodies, they can "borrow" or "possess" planetary bodies. They can also act as conduits for the invisible outer planets and stellar narrativium. Research shows that natal and transiting Nodes are activated during incidents of spirit possession. The Nodal axis has the potential to act as a conduit for things other than souls, including non-corporeal entities, spirits, daimons, demons, angelic beings, planetary intelligences, etc. The Nodes are capable of moving thoughts and thought-forms around, with or without consent. Think about the last time a song replayed repeatedly in your mind, or when an idea got stuck in your head, and see if there were any transits to your natal Nodes or contacts from the transiting Nodes. The Moon has a great deal to do with the constant flow of thoughts through the mind, and the Moon's Nodes may be complicit in specific types of mental activity.

- The Nodes take center stage every five to six lunar cycles during eclipses, when they appear to "swallow" the Sun or Moon. The periodicity of eclipses can be erratic, but there are generally two sets of eclipses per year, with one solar and one lunar eclipse per set. There may be as many as six eclipses in a calendar year because of minor annular eclipses that produce three eclipses over a 6-week intervals, or when the Nodes are in the Cancer-Capricorn axis and create sets of eclipses in January, June, and December of a single calendar year. The Nodes are most dramatic when they are visibly eating the light of the Sun and Moon during partial and total eclipses.

- The natal Nodal Axis shows the path of the individual's soul-thread within the collective. This relates to the rabbinical quote: *souls are like the wick of a candle, many threads bound together.* The Nodal Axis is the conduit for this candlewick of entwined souls. The natal sign and house axis of the Nodes shows how the soul is entwined and woven into the tapestry of the collective, and how and where the individual intersects with the collective.

- The Nodes make a complete circuit of the zodiac in 18.5 years, a Metonic Cycle. Nodes take about 2 1/2 years to travel through a zodiac sign, and participate in 8 to 12 eclipses in that zodiacal axis.

- The Nodes create a backward-moving axis in the zodiac that mimics the churning of the cosmos. The life-churning events that coincide with eclipses demonstrate this effect, as do planets that occupy the bendings (square the Nodes) by natal placement or progressions.

- A planet conjunct the North Node is on a rise, the king of the hill. The North Node makes a planet's needs, wants and desires more intense and gives the planet a platform for fulfilling those wants and desires. A planet conjunct the South Node is in a ditch or a trough. The planet can't function, can't see or get what it needs. In a natal chart, a planet-South Node conjunction indicates that the individual may become focused on "digesting" planet-related material. There may be some fate-related imperative to fulfill matters in the current life that were incomplete in a past life.

Although I am not fond of keyword lists, here's a list associated with the North and South Nodes:

North Node	South Node
Rahu	Ketu
Caput Draconis	Cauda Draconis
Head	Tail
Ingests	Digests
Dharma	Karma

Ketu has a bad reputation for excesses & indulgences. It may indicate how and where people lose their way in life. Since Ketu has no brain it tends to be reliant on instinctive and sensory modes of expression. It's the gut of the Nodal dragon and, not to be indelicate, is the exit hatch for karmic poo. Let's reframe this as "the end results of a process or digestion." The end result may not be disgusting—that depends on what's been digested and how the person processed it.

Conscious effort is required to lift Ketu into higher spiritualized forms of expression. When that happens, Ketu has the potential to be close to the divine. Ketu's end-products may be the exaltation of a soul in the material form of an incarnation. This side of Ketu is associated with holy hermits or ascetics who choose an existence of fasting, prayer and meditation. They detach from the material world through denial of the flesh. This extreme self-denial is a means for releasing the poo of materiality, fully exploring the soul, and exalting the spirit.

Western culture has little value for people who renounce the world. To obtain a more modern context, reflect on the idea of "the end result of a process." For example, consider the writer who hunches over his or her computer for days, weeks, and months, barely eating, sleeping, or functioning normally until the book is complete. It is an obsessive but productive process. The same thing can happen to an actor or dancer preparing for a new show. The performer thinks about nothing but that role for days or weeks until the show opens. A scientist or researcher may engage in an obsessive quest for discovery. An athlete may train for years to win contests of physical skill, strength, and endurance. The material aspects of life—eating, sleeping, bathing, house-keeping, relationships, socializing—are re-prioritized as secondary to the primary obsession and may be neglected. The end result of all this effort (a book, a performance, a new formula or understanding of natural science, an Olympic gold medal) is the culmination of a process, the individual's quest to digest the inspiration and process it into a desirable outcome or achievement.

For some, a Ketu obsession may only last as long as it takes to fulfill a single project. For others, Ketu obsessions can last a lifetime. For full disclosure, this book was edited and prepared for publication while Saturn was making a direct station within a few degrees of my natal Ketu. There are examples of life-long obsessions from natal planet-Ketu conjunctions in Chapter 11: Chart Samples.

The more common Western understanding of Ketu skews toward excessive indulgences of vices. Planets connected to the Ketu ditch are *needy*. If the needs aren't fulfilled, Ketu instinctively tries to fill up on substitutes that are inappropriate but accessible: too much alcohol, too many drugs, too much spending, too much sex, gang membership, extremist rhetoric, etc. This might be associated with karma, but it could also be an excess of a certain behavior that keeps the brain's pleasure center lit up like a Christmas tree—the sensible portion of the Platonic soul that relates to the physical senses. Ketu is the dragon's tail—it thrashes around and isn't easy to control. Some people might call that karma, but it could be hormones or brain chemistry in overdrive. Sometimes karma is not a useful explanation, and it could easily get turned into an excuse. Conflating excesses with past lives or karma isn't always a helpful thing to say to a client; while there may be karmic overtones, the clients have to deal with issues in the here-and-now.

The South Node should be included when formatting a natal chart. It's easy to miss significant contacts to Ketu when it isn't displayed or printed. The North and South Nodes function in tandem as an axis and create a dynamic link between opposing houses.

The transiting Nodes are fully capable of inhabiting natal planetary bodies during conjunctions, too. When the transiting North Node conjuncts a natal planet, it becomes more like an antenna that picks up all kinds of signals and messages. It may attract another person who embodies the qualities of that planet, or events reflective of that planet's significations. The transiting Nodes and eclipses generate an overload of activity that is characteristic to the planet, sign, and house.

Conjunctions to natal planets by the transiting South Node can trigger fairly obsessive efforts to cope with and process planet-sign-house related situations and events. A transiting South Node conjunction can make the effects of a natal (or progressed) planet more unpredictable, uncontrollable, or excessive. Since the Nodes are invisible and ghost-like, the best way to observe their influence is when they are conjunct a familiar planet or chart axis point.

The Nodal Bendings
A planet that is square the Nodes is said to be at "the bendings." A natal planet square the Nodes is a life-time dynamic. There may also be temporary periods when the transiting Nodes square a natal or progressed planet. A variation is the progressed Nodes squaring a progressed planet. The individual is compelled to move forward (a North Node quality) in order to effectively process (South Node) issues that are specific to the planet, sign and house. Nodal squares often churn up issues from a person's past that must be resolved before the person can proceed with the next phase of life.

A progressed Nodal square to progressed Mars can last for some years and trigger arguments, quarrels, angers, attacks, and frustrations linked to a repressed libido. A young male client experienced a great deal of difficulty with explosive bursts of misdirected anger for a four-year period when his progressed Nodes squared progressed Mars. He made noticeable improvements by attending regular therapy sessions with a counselor. Identifying the sources of his anger and developing ways of managing it helped him move into the next phase of his life. He established a fulfilling, mature relationship with a woman that provided an outlet for his sexual nature. The combination of anger therapy, the relationship, and regular sex helped him move past his Mars issues, which faded away at the Nodes and Mars progressed away from the exact square.

Transiting Nodal squares to natal planets last for a few weeks, but the planet-related issues they stir up require essentially the same process: recognition and identification of the core problem; debates, discussions or consultations about the condition; followed by decisions and applied solutions. If the natal planet is well-placed and has favorable aspects, this process may be hardly noticeable. If the natal planet is badly placed and/or has nasty aspects, a transiting Nodal square can trigger unpleasant situations and lesser-evil type decision-making. A higher degree of courage and self-honesty is required. If the square passes and no substantive changes have been made, the situation has the potential to return with a vengeance down the road when the planet is activated by eclipses, outer planet transits, or another Nodal square nine years later.

Judging the Nodes in a birth chart

There are many ways of considering the natal Nodes. These are the things I look for:

- Are the Nodes in an important house axis in the natal chart?
- Is a Node conjunct a natal planet?
- Is the Nodal Axis conjunct a natal axis (Asc-Dsc or MC-IC)?
- Do the Nodes receive a major aspect from any natal planets?
- Do the Nodes form an axis for a configuration like a Grand Cross, T-Square, White or Black Dragon (Kite), or Mystic Rectangle?
- Was the person born immediately before, during, or after an eclipse? For more details, where were the solar and lunar eclipses preceding and following birth? Were they total or partial eclipses? Are there any natal planetary conjunctions to those degrees? If there were eclipses after a person was born, at what age will they be active by progression?
- Are the Nodes relatively hidden in the chart, cadent, with only minor aspects?

Mantras for Remediating Nodes

Although it is tangential to the focus of this text, I'm including Sanskrit mantras for the Nodes, as these are somewhat hard to find.

Rahu: Om Govinda Varapatraye Namaha. Twice blessed by Vishnu, container of the lord's grace. Worthy of respect.

Ketu: Om Mahodaraya Namaha. Large belly, Ganesha. Vast capacity, great power, can give any amount in any way of anything.[1]

There are other Rahu and Ketu mantras, but I've used these two with very good results. These mantras are particularly helpful during slow planet transits of the natal Nodes and for minimizing the negative effects of eclipses. They are also helpful for minimizing the obsessions, phobias, and bad habits linked to natal planet-Node conjunctions. For best effects, repeat the mantra 108 times per day for seven days.

Mercury's Cycles and Spirals

The Nodes are comfortable in mutable signs, and Mercury rules two of these—Gemini and Virgo. Mercury is the most changeable planet and mutable sign ruler. Mutable signs promote the flexibility needed to make continual adjustments and tweaks through the tides of life. They represent the ebb and flow of life that the individual experiences in a communal environment that is ever-churning and impermanent.

Mercury's caduceus was given to him in myth by the Lord of the Underworld so he could travel easily between the realms of the underworld, earth, and the realm of the immortal gods. It has two snakes twining up column. These equate to the body's meridians, the Ida and Pingala. Sometimes the caduceus is surmounted by a pair of wings, a symbol of the flying soul. The spirals are reminiscent of the patterns of Saros Cycles created by eclipse families. The first eclipse in the group takes place near the North or South Pole. Each subsequent eclipse in the family rises or descends from the position of the first eclipse. Over hundreds of years, the Saros eclipse families create several enormous spirals wrapped around the Earth in space-time, moving in opposite directions. This, too, mimics the churning movement of the stars and planets.

Mercury is always close to the Sun, so when the planet is visible, it's fairly close to the horizon during its eastern/rising or western/setting phases. It has a speedy regenerative cycle compared to the other planets. Mercury is like the Moon of the Sun and his retrogrades are much more like eclipses; the same is true of Venus. When Mercury retrogrades, it orbits in front of the Sun and is swallowed by the beams, disappearing from view. After the retrograde ends, a "new Mercury" rises before the Sun in the pre-dawn glow. Within a few weeks, Mercury appears closer to the Sun again, and soon disappears behind the body of the Sun. This is a "full Mercury." Some days later Mercury begins to appear after sundown as an evening star. The orbit of Venus is identical in astronomical movement but slower, and she retrogrades once every year and a half. Gary Caton's book on Mercury does an excellent job of digging into the specifics of Mercury phases and retrograde patterns.[2]

The interpretation of natal Mercury is challenging because the planet's phases are unique and Mercury wears so many different hats. It dies and is reborn three to four times each year as a morning star. Death is a cheesy card trick for Mercury. Joanne Conman associates the Set with Mercury.³ Although in myths Set is a god of chaos, he's shown protecting the solar boat of Ra from the ravenous attack of Typhon, the monster than wants to eat time. Early depictions of Seth have an anteater's head on the body of a man. It's easy to imagine Set poking his long nose where it doesn't belong! Later images of Seth feature a more dog-like face. Mercury is the magpie of the planets and it has picked up all kinds of meanings and attributions through the past 2,000 years. This planet has a myriad of astrological significations, many jobs, and many names.

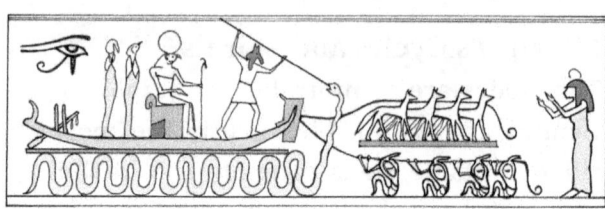

Set at the front of the boat attacking Typhon with a spear. EH

Mercury's orbit involves churning and turning. This makes him more Node-like *and* star-like than any of the other planets. Both the Nodes and Mercury have a heightened capacity to partake of stellar narrativium and channel stellar meanings through conjunctions. Mercury's stations or combustion phases often coincide with Full and New Moons and eclipses. Mercury is a master of disguises, too. Consider what might happen if a Node was conjunct Mercury *and* a fixed star. It wouldn't bother Mercury to have its body borrowed by the Node, and the star's energy would be funneled into a distinctive manifestation or story line. This precise aspect is explored in Syd Barrett's chart in Chapter 11, page 121.

The Psychopompos At Play
Mercury performs role of psychopompos by leading souls to realm of the dead. The caduceus is a miniature representation of the World Tree, along which the various realms of the gods, the living, and the dead are arranged. It's a magic wand that allows Mercury, Hermes-Thoth, and Hermes Trismegistus to travel to all of these realms as a messenger of the gods and a guide to souls.

Mercury facilitates the transmigration process. A significant clue to this soul-shepherding function is Mercury's joy in the first house. Joy is an ancient form of house-related accidental dignity. He conducts, reflects, bends, diverts, distorts, and modulates solar light. In the metaphysical cosmos, stars and souls are etheric fire—light! Mercury is the prism that gets the light from here to there and back again during his erratic path. The Egyptian depiction of Seth at the prow of the solar boat and the role of Hermes Trismegistus as the focal deity of the Hermetic soul cult should make this point very clear.

"Joy" is a house-related dignity. The visible planets perform well in these houses, which are assigned by sect and by each planet's qualities.

All things on Earth exist in the sub-lunar realm. Celestial influences are channeled and filtered by the Moon and modulated by the Nodes. The integrated deity, Hermes-Thoth, combines Mercury with Thoth, a Moon god associated with the underworld, hermetic magic, and the maintenance of cosmic order. This multi-cultural merger gives a big honking tip-off about the unified function of these planets in soul travel. Mercury and the Moon are natal significators of the soular light in play at birth.

Mercury is the most playful and mischievous Greek god. Divine play is a critical concept personified by the Hindus as Lila, "she who plays". The creation of the cosmos is called *lila*, the play of God. Lila is an important concept in the traditional worship of Krishna (a youthful prankster avatar of Vishnu). Lila plays as Shiva-Nataraja performs the Tandava-Lasya dance to destroy and re-create the world. Vishnu is sometimes conflated with Brahman.

> "The world is a mere spontaneous creation of Brahman. It is a Lila, or sport, of Brahman. It is created out of Bliss, by Bliss and for Bliss. Lila indicates a spontaneous sportive activity of Brahman as distinguished from a self-conscious volitional effort. The concept of Lila signifies freedom as distinguished from necessity."[4]
> —Ram Shanker Misra

> "In the Hindu view of nature, then, all forms are relative, fluid and ever-changing maya, conjured up by the great magician of the divine play. The world of maya changes continuously, because the divine lila is a rhythmic, dynamic play. The dynamic force of the play is karma, an important concept of Indian thought. Karma means "action". It is the active principle of the play, the total universe in action, where everything is dynamically connected with everything else."[5]
> —Fritjof Capra

Lila is comparable to the Western theological position of Pandeism, which describes the Universe as God taking a physical form in order to experience the interplay between the elements of the Universe. A key difference is that the Greeks conceptualized Necessity/Ananke as a co-author of creation, whereas the Hindu version posits Brahma's creation of the cosmos as spontaneous play and bliss.

The meanings of the planet Mercury encompass both ideological positions. He is a thief, trickster, a bloody genius, a mad scientist, and the thrice-great magician. He can be a child, adult, or elder, male or female. He conducts the music of the spheres. The Egyptian Seth was chaotic, beset with a permanent case of divine madness, but he was also the guardian and protector of the Sun who ensured that time endured.

Heliacal Rising Stars and Doryphories

Astrologers can assemble the clues about the games Mercury was playing with soular light on a birth date. The Egyptians ordered their society around heliacal rising stars. When this is integrated into the clues about soular light, the heliacal rising star puts some English, a distinctive spin, on what Mercury is doing on a particular day. A significant star conjunct the natal Ascendant is an additional factor, if present. The condition of star-related planets may be considered as a secondary influence.

Doryphories are a further clue to a soul's purpose. A doryphory is a spear-bearer, or as I like to call them, a spearchuckers, borrowed from Dr. Oliver "Spearchucker" Jones, a surgeon and football ringer in the book **M*A*S*H**[4] by Richard Hooker. [6]

Spearchucker planets travel in a procession ahead the Sun, like the majorettes and marching band precede the mayor (Sun) riding in a convertible and waving at people. Oriental planets are *akhs* in the Akhet—most effective and freshly hatched from the cosmic combustion chamber. Doryphories indicate a person's most ardent capabilities, the qualities and skills that will be most dynamic and prominent.

Bloody Samurai, Meiji-era artist 1868-1912.

A simple trick for spotting spear-chuckers is to turn the chart so the natal Sun is near the left thumb, in the position of an Ascendant. If there are visible planets above the Sun within roughly 45 degrees, they are spearchuckers. If a spearchucker is conjunct a star, then it's got some English, a specialized spin to it. The closer a spearchucker is to the Sun, the more its traits and qualities are subsumed into the personality. The person will see that trait or ability as inseparable from who they are. A planet is combust or *in the beams* if it is within 12 degrees ahead or behind the Sun, although some use an 8 degree orb for combustion.

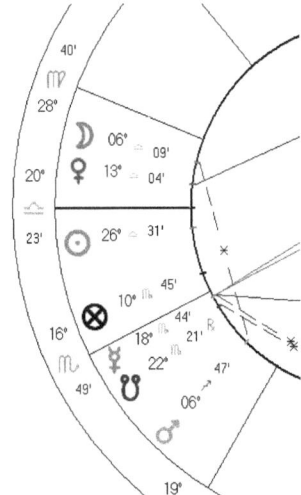

The Moon and Venus are spear-bearers in poet Arthur Rimbaud's natal chart. Rimbaud was born shortly before sunrise.

Spearchuckers are oriental or east-rising, and express themselves in a super-yang, externalized, assertive manner. Hellenic and classical astrologers have more refined or specific qualifications for doryphories. I've found that a planet or planets that are 12 to 20 degrees ahead of the Sun at sunrise are effective spearchuckers and give a good idea about the first-foot-forward traits the person will have.

The list of soul-purpose indicators should include the heliacal rising star; a star conjunct the Ascendant (if there is one), and doryphories. Mercury, Moon, North and South Nodes (and any stars conjunct these) may also delineate factors of an individual's soul purpose. Sign and house help determine how these factors are likely to manifest. Dane Rudhyar's chart in Chapter 11, page 128, provides an excellent example of powerful doryphories.

Progressed Mercury

Mercury may offer further information about the soul's journey through an incarnation. If Mercury makes natal or secondary progressed major aspects to the Nodes, it's a red flag that something's churning with the incarnation. This may represent a special connection between the individual and the collective, the cultural environment, or zeitgeist. It may indicate the individual has an important but possibly invisible impact on the lives of others. The Nodes are shadow planets, so visibility or prominence isn't guaranteed. Effects may not be immediately obvious.

A person with a significant Mercury-Node contact could be a Pied Piper leading others where they wouldn't go without that guidance, however subtle. A natal Mercury-Node aspect extends its influence through the entire life, while a progressed Mercury-Node contact influences a specific period of time. Consider Mercury's relationship to the sign's ruler and meaning of the house, as well as houses that Mercury rules and its aspects to other planets in the chart.

Mercury will retrograde at some time before, during, or after date of birth. If Mercury retrogrades after birth, the retrograde will show up in secondary progressions. Other types of progressions will show Mercury stations but in a different time scale; this section focuses on secondary progressions as they're notably accurate for predicting significant life changes. Use an ephemeris to chart Mercury's activities during the months before and after birth; it's good to anticipate this event. Progressed Mercury retrogrades may coincide with career changes, professional leaps, and finding the right niche for talents and skills.

John Lennon, a lead singer and co-songwriter with Paul McCartney in The Beatles, is a prime example of the impact of progressed Mercury. His natal Mercury was in Scorpio behind his Libra Sun in the evening star phase. It made a progressed opposition to Uranus when he was around 16-years old, precisely when he started playing with a band and meeting the boys who would eventually become The Beatles. His progressed Mercury turned retrograde when he was 24-years old in 1964, the year that The Beatles were launched into super-stardom and toured in the United States. When progressed Mercury Rx repeated the opposition to Uranus in 1969, his interest eroded and the band broke up within a year. The connections between natal, progressed, and 1980 solar return Mercury were quite ominous. He was killed about two months after his 40th birthday. The list of well-known people who made career changes and leaps during a progressed Mercury retrograde or direct stations is substantial, and includes Michael Jackson, Madonna, Judy Garland, Lucille Ball, and Jimmy Fallon.

Progressed Mercury stations always coincide with significant life events. There is no guarantee that the station will lead to good things, though. The natal condition and aspects of Mercury must be taken into account along with progressed aspects. House position can be indicative of the area of life where the changes will take place. A divorced female client had a progressed Mercury retrograde that had completed a direct station and returned to its natal degree in her fifth house of children. Her child reached 18 years of age, which freed her from constant contact and child support battles with the child's father, who was (in her view) an annoying pest. With this onerous obstacle removed, she moved to a new location and got a new job. The karmic overtones in that situation are very clear, as karma can involve raising a child, taking care of family members, or resolving a problematic past life relationship. Sometimes leaving a relationship is good karma.

Mercury retrogrades last around 20 to 25 days; roughly 20 to 25 years by progression. There is invariably some learning or growth process that takes place during these years. Taking the time to figure out the beginning and ending times of a progressed Mercury retrograde can help flesh out the big picture for a client. Major aspects to other planets Mercury makes during his churning process can be highly significant. When the aspect repeats some years later, the individual will have reach a turning point. This is a chance to resolve or advance from the conditions put in place during the previous aspect.

Mercury. Wood engraving by Jonnard after W. B. Richmond, 1866. Wiki Commons

Ascertain the significant degrees of Mercury's movements, including Mercury's conjunctions to the Sun, its retrograde and direct stations, and any triple conjunctions to a Mag 1 fixed star. Triple planetary aspects during the course of a progressed retrograde portend significant exchanges, interactions, and changes of awareness related to signs and houses. Progressed Mercury retrogrades may revive or recycle unresolved issues or past life material; the direct station should bring about a resolution. The resolution period may take two to three years as secondary progressions are planets in slow motion. The houses that Mercury occupies and rules are areas of life that will be affected, the zodiac sign shows the circumstances and context of a situation, and aspects show the reasons—who or what is involved and influential.

The meaning of a progressed Mercury retrograde won't come with a big blinking label to tell you how it will manifest. It may be subtle and require detective work. The astrologer may have to evaluate progressed Mercury over long periods of time by observing events, behavioral changes, and lifestyle changes in the client's life. An astrologer's job includes pondering the mysteries of life, and this is a big one. Begin by asking the questions: what was Mercury doing at the time of birth? Where, when, and how did he move the cheese?

Three Major Natal Axes

There are three major axes in a natal chart: the Ascendant-Descendent axis, the Midheaven-Nadir axis, and the Nodal axis. These represent Time, Space, and Motion. Three axes are required to form a cube, or for a soul to take shape and manifest in a body. A natal chart may have additional oppositions formed by planets, or by planets and stars. A natal planetary conjunction to *any* axis point is important, especially if the axis is conjunct a fixed star.

Depicting a natal chart on a piece of paper requires compromises. Visible dimensions are lost. The north-south axis is merged with the prime vertical to produce the Midheaven-Nadir axis, squashing the chart flat. However, other dimensions sneak into the chart through the Nodal axis, oppositions, and contra-parallels.

Earth is the sublunary realm in ancient thought. The influences of all of the planets and stars are filtered by the Moon before trickling down to Earth. The Nodes are the Moon's points of intersection with the ecliptic, so they, too, assist with the job of filtering things from the solar system and beyond. It's a universal axis that has the potential to act as a conduit for planetary and stellar themes. Whether they perform this task or not greatly depends on whether they're in contact with natal planets. A natal chart must show evidence of this quality for the potential to manifest.

Visible planets give a more obvious show-and-tell when manifesting through the Nodes. The invisible outer planets—Uranus, Neptune, and Pluto—are powerful, collective, and sometimes subversive. They rarely do favors for the individual. Rather, they draw the person into an experience that relates to the greater collective. They may manifest in productive ways if the person has the capacity, intellect, and ambition to channel their abilities and obsessions into fruitful activities. It helps if the person has visible planets in good aspect to the invisible planets, as this allows the person to develop methods for channeling these remote energies in tangible personalized ways.

Challenging aspects from invisible planets to the Nodes can drag people through a bush backward, as though evil blind fate or an angry god is targeting them for punishment. Liz Greene wrote about this effect in **The Astrology of Fate**[7] (1984). Another excellent book on the nature of the outer planets is **The Gods of Change**[8] by Howard Sasportas (1989). Invisible planet conjunctions to either Node are no joking matter. They can be intensely difficult to process because of the invisibility factor of both the Nodes and the outer planets.

Jim Morrison of the Doors and Jimmy Page of Led Zepplin were born a few weeks apart in December 1943 and January 1944 with Pluto conjunct the North Node in Leo. The Doors and Led Zepplin were musical eruptions in the fabric of the social collective. The genius of their music continues to have an impact on younger musicians. But they also exemplify the Pluto effect as they rammed head-first into peril by dabbling into the occult, by challenging taboos, and exceeding boundaries.

Their charts make it clear why Morrison died and Page survived, albeit pounded into a reformed life by the tragic death of band-mate John "Bonzo" Bohnam. Morrison's Nodes and Pluto straddle his Ascendant-Descendant axis and make a Grand Cross with the Moon and Venus. The voracious South Node is on his Ascendant, and his ferocious appetite for drugs and sex was his undoing. Page's Pluto-North Node conjunction is cadent in the ninth house. The Nodal axis forms a Mystic Rectangle with Venus and Mars. The cadent location of the Pluto-North Node conjunction with trines and sextiles made it easier to integrate more effectively, but he still took much harm from it. An additional ameliorating factor is that Page had some interest in astrology and even had his critical chart significators embroidered on his clothing. The ninth house signifies divination and prophecy; his awareness of his natal Pluto-Node conjunction may have helped somewhat. (Chart data: Morrison, born Dec 8, 1943, 11:55 am EST, Melbourne, Florida, RR: AA; Page, born Jan 9, 1944, 4:17 am BST, Heston, England, RR: AA.)

The birth charts of Morrison and Page are well-worth examining for placements that contributed to their life paths. Their enormous initial impact and continuing influences on music and culture make their charts fine examples of *djet* time-event vectors reverberating for many years. They are also poster-children for why using invisible outer planets as sign rulers is inadvisable. Toxic substances are attributed to these planets: nitroglycerin (Uranus); chemical acids (Neptune); and radioactive material (Pluto). Their effects can be tremendous and they are relevant significators for contemporary technologies, but it's counter-productive to put them in charge of anything, especially as an Ascendant ruler. If a demon is given a job, it's much more likely to pop out of the box and do mischief. The average person is not well-conditioned to deal with invisible entities.

Chapter 10

Draconic Charts and Other Portals

Draconic or dragon charts are a 20th century method from the Hamberg School of Astrology, founded by Alfred Witte in October, 1925. This branch became known as Uranian Astrology in the United States. Reinhold Ebertin was a student of the school and re-dubbed its methods as "Cosmobiology."

A draconic chart is created by shifting the natal North Node to 0° Aries and then adjusting the positions of all of the other planets and chart points by the same amount of degrees. Dragon charts aren't used very often but can be a gold mine of information about the life focus and purpose of a soul's incarnation. Draconic contacts give pointers to life lessons, potential accomplishments, and challenges. These charts may be combined with transits, and are used in synastry to show karmic links to other individuals in a person's life.

0° Aries is the fiducial (starting) point of the Zodiac. It symbolizes collective awakening, renewal, the potency of life's potentials, and conscious awareness. As the Sun passes 0° Aries, the hours of light become greater than the hours of darkness in the northern hemisphere. A draconic chart reframes a person's natal chart into a collective soul-related context.

The North Node represents the Dragon's head and instinctive ingestion. A dragon chart shows what the soul is most likely to be drawn to and ingest from the collective. Contacts between the natal chart and dragon chart show where the individual has the potential for leadership and discovery. A leader in this context may simply be a person who figures out how to do something efficiently and successfully, and is able to share these methods with others who follow in that path. A leader can be a role model or path finder with no obvious followers.

How to use a Draconic Chart
The planetary positions in a Draconic chart are used like fixed stars—only conjunctions between draconic and natal planets and axis points are considered. Tight orbs are preferable. There may be very few conjunctions. It's rare to find more than three or four contacts between natal and draconic charts. Less is more! It takes careful pondering to interpret these contacts. Examining transits to natal-draconic conjunctions expands the basis for interpretation. The events

and reactions to those events will help elucidate the meaning of the contact. A draconic contact is a hot-spot that remains active throughout a person's entire life span.

It is preferable to use the True Node to calculate the natal and dragon charts. In Solar Fire, open a New Chart Data Entry box and input natal data. On the right side of the box, look for the Zodiac toggle. It will probably read "Tropical." Scroll down and click on "Draconic". Set up a biwheel with the tropical natal chart as the inner wheel and draconic chart as the outer wheel. There are two draconic sample charts presented in Chapter 11, pages 150-158.

Antiscia

If you haven't worked with antiscia, think "Bond, James Bond." Antiscia* are like surveillance bugs or hidden cameras. Each natal planet has antiscion bugs planted in two other signs and houses so it can witness what's going on there. It's a spy device for intel grabs, a fly on the wall. Antiscia can form secret aspects to other planets, so if planets have no major natal aspects, they might have sub-rosa contacts by way of the antiscia.

Antiscia are the alternate point in the zodiac *with the same amount of sunlight.* In order to calculate antiscia, divide the zodiac in half from Cancer to Capricorn (the Solstitial Axis). The two hemispheres mirror one another. Each planet resonates with its position in the mirror above or below the equinoctial border. If a natal planet is at 25° Scorpio, it is 35 degrees away from 0° Capricorn. Its antiscion is 5° Aquarius, 35 degrees away from 0° Capricorn in the other direction. The hours of daylight when the Sun is transiting 25° Scorpio and 5° Aquar-

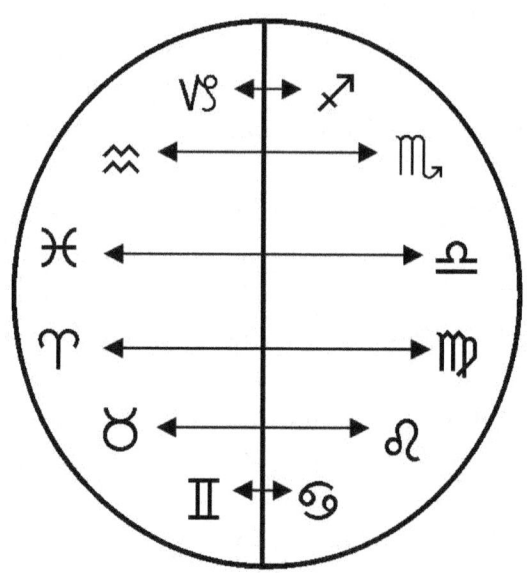

Beholding Signs

---

*Antiscia (pronounced *an-Ti-sha*) refers to all antiscia. Antiscions is plural and is used when more than one but not all are being referenced. Antiscion (*an-Ti-shun*) is the singular noun.

ius are the same. If a natal planet is at 14° Taurus, it is 46 degrees away from 0° Cancer. Its antiscion is at 16° Leo, 46 degrees away from 0° Cancer in the opposite direction. The hours of daylight at 14° Taurus and 16° Leo are the same. Contra-antiscions are in opposition to the antiscions, so these sneaky reflections of light create more axes in the chart.

Some astrology software programs will do the calculations for you, but once the concept is grasped, its pretty easy to calculate in your head. Learn the six base pairs:

      Aries reflects into Virgo (and vice versa)
      Taurus reflects into Leo (and vice versa)
      Gemini reflects into Cancer (and vice versa)
      Libra reflects into Pisces (and vice versa)
      Scorpio reflects into Aquarius (and vice versa)
      Sagittarius reflects into Capricorn (and vice versa)

The antiscia and contra-antiscia may form secret conjunctions to Draconic chart positions. Since antiscia are reflections of light, antiscion contacts to draconic charts may show singular opportunities to learn karmic lessons through contact with others. Antiscion reflections may involve a level of discomfort. Let's consider two imaginary people, Sheila and Ralph. Sheila thinks Ralph has irritating traits and behaviors! Then she discovers that his natal Mars is conjunct her natal Mars antiscion and her Draconic Moon. Sheila then realizes that she, too, sometimes manifests those traits or behaviors. Ralph's Mars mirrors Sheila's Mars right back at her. Mutual antiscion and draconic contacts between personal charts have the potential to reflect and magnify positive behaviors, too. People who share these types of contacts bring out the best in each other. It's common to find these kinds of positive-reinforcement contacts in the charts of happily married couples.

Prince William and Kate Middleton's shared antiscia and draconic contacts are astounding and show exceptional potential for mutual positive reinforcement and understanding. Sometimes couples with very few mutual natal chart contacts have a plethora of antiscia or draconic contacts. The partners see things in one another that nobody else sees, and that's why they're drawn to one another.

Antiscia and draconic placements are activated through transits and progressions just like natal placements. As points of reflected planetary light, antiscia don't convey stellar energy, but they can and do form aspect relationships with natal planets.* These secretive relationships can go a long way toward explaining skills and abilities a person may possess. They may be activated during significant events where there are no visible transits to natal planets.

In this manner, antiscia act like portals of hidden planetary energy within a natal chart. But they aren't the only portals that were used by ancient astrologers. For more in-depth information about antisca, see **Antiscia: Secrets in the Mirror**.[1]

Hellenic Lots

The Lots, or Arabic Parts, are esoteric portals that show where chance circumstances will arise through the machinations of planetary spirits and messengers (like angels) related to the Lot's planet.[2] Lots are doorways that can be activated by transits and eclipses. An activated Lot may result in specific events, meetings, or *eureka!* moments of awareness, discovery and invention. In the earliest Hellenic system, the Lots were limited and related to the seven visible planets. Most astrologers used day and night formulae to calculate the lots, depending on whether the birth chart was diurnal or nocturnal. Chris Brennan's essay on the Lots is essential reading on the topic. His Lot meanings are paraphrased below.[3]

The Hellenic Lots are:
Lot of the Moon (Part of Fortune or PF)
    Day: ASC + Moon—Sun. Night: ASC + Sun—Moon.
Lot of the Sun (Part of Spirit or PS)
    Day: ASC + Sun—Moon. Night: ASC + Moon—Sun.

The remaining planetary Lots utilize the Lots of the Sun and Moon (Part of Spirit or PS and Part of Fortune or PF, respectively) in their formulae that relate to their jobs as sect team members. The diurnal sect planets are the Sun, Jupiter and Saturn; the nocturnal sect planets are the Moon, Venus and Mars. Mercury is a neutral party.

Lot of Mercury (Necessity-Ananke)
    Day: ASC + PF—Mercury. Night: ASC + Mercury—PF
Lot of Venus (Eros)
    Day: ASC + Venus—PS. Night: ASC + PS—Venus.

---

*Firmicus Maternus states in **Mathesis**[4] that antiscia can form aspects. Some astrologers, however, only use antiscion conjunctions. In the past few years, these have picked up the nickname of "ninja conjunctions" because they're not visible on the surface but jump out at the astrologer who looks for them.

Lot of Mars (Courage)
    Day: ASC + PF—Mars. Night: ASC + Mars—PF
Lot of Jupiter (Victory-Nike)
    Day: ASC + Jupiter—PS. Night: ASC + PS—Jupiter
Lots of Saturn (Nemesis)
    Day: ASC + PF—Saturn. Night: ASC + Saturn—PF

Lot Meanings

The Lot of the Sun or Part of Spirit (PS) shows what is becoming or gaining energy in the birth chart. In a diurnal chart, the PS shows efforts and outcomes, particularly relating to social, professional, and intellectual endeavors. In nocturnal charts, the PS is more passive and reflects state of mind.

The Lot of the Moon or Part of Fortune (PF) shows which Light is being reduced in energy by calculating the Lot from the active to passive sect light. The PF shows what is available and accessible in the person's environment. The person doesn't generate or create what is gained through the PF. This Lot shows the condition of the body and health, material property and goods, along with the possibility for pleasure, love, and enjoyment. If badly aspected, it can show diseases. Like the Moon it reflects and gathers incoming thoughts, environmental influences and material goods. In this sense, the PF is passive, but in relation to material goods, it is tangible.

The Lot of Mercury—Ananke or Necessity. Ananke/Necessity has been mentioned numerous times in earlier chapters as an important component of fate and destiny. Necessity involves obstacles the individual must overcome in order to make progress. Natal planetary aspects to the Lot of Necessity show the relative ease or difficulty a person will experience in overcoming life's obstacles. Difficult aspects signal arguments and contentions, while good aspects promote helpful exchanges and positive exchanges. The Lot shows whether the person will be a leader or a subordinate, whether the person will be able to get good jobs or struggle to get a good job with good pay, and whether the person is greedy or generous. Mixed aspects create mixed situations with this Lot. Since it is named for a critical force in the cosmos, study this Lot carefully.

The Lot of Venus—Love or Eros. This lot relates to the inner psychological nature of the individual and circumstances that foster desire and attraction. It shows how and where relationships begin, success or failure in marriage, single or multiple marriages, and sexual preferences. Good aspects indicate solid relationships, while contacts to the malefic planets and/or bad aspects indicate possible scandals and troublesome relationships.

The Lot of Mars—Courage or Fortitudo. This Lot relates to military or professional circumstances where aggression or assertiveness are needed, and shows (by sign and house) where the individual is most likely to encounter impulsive behavior, attacks and betrayals. It shows whether the person will be a bully or be bullied by others. The natal element gives this Lot its traits: fire is quick to anger and quick to forget. Earth is slow to anger and slow to forget. Water is moodier and insults can turn to grudges and bottled-up resentment. Air shows verbal arguments and intellectual rather than physical battles.

The Lot of Jupiter—Victory or Nike. This is the Lot of faith and trust, partnerships and potential success. When well-aspected, this Lot indicates high status, beneficial alliances and wealth. It may also relate to strong religious beliefs and spirituality, a philosophical nature, and benefits or status that come through others, particularly through inheritances or inherited family status. With good planets and aspects, it increases the ability to enjoy positive outcomes. With difficult planets or bad aspects, it shows gains followed by losses and difficulty in improving one's status and finances. The Lot's element and mode show the types of conquests the individual will be involved in, his or her values, goals and ambitions.

The Lot of Saturn—Retribution or Nemesis. This Lot shows what is hidden and concealed, banished, confined, isolated, or imprisoned. It indicates a source of losses and sorrows and the quality of death. It shows how the person may be constrained by life circumstances or troublesome issues. Benefic aspects offer a means of escape and shorter periods of constraint. Malefic aspects make problems worse and extend limitations. A good aspect from Saturn reduces hardships and makes it easier to cope; the problems or hardships could actually become advantageous and more easily endured over time.

Singer Whitney Houston's chart provides an example of a high-functioning Lot of Nemesis. (See chart, page 120) Her natal Saturn is at 19° Aquarius in the 12th house, and her Lot of Nemesis is at 19° Libra in the 7th house. Saturn trines its own Lot, and the Lot gets an opposition from her Moon-Jupiter conjunction in Aries, while Saturn has oppositions to her Leo Sun and Venus.

Houston achieved global fame after appearing in the film **The Bodyguard** in 1992. A few fans turned into stalkers. Houston was obliged to implement home security measures and deterrents, hire bodyguards, and work with members of law enforcement. These incidents were frightening and uncomfortable for her; she became a "bird in a golden cage" at her high-security mansion in Atlanta. Her accumulated wealth made her confinement luxurious (Jupiter) and fame encouraged law enforcement authorities to be exceptionally cooperative.

Her Lot of Necessity describes her death in detail. She died in a bathtub, a confined 12th-house type space, at the Beverly Wiltshire Hotel, a luxurious Libra-type establishment (12th house locations can be transient). It was a sudden death, signified by the Lot of Nemesis in a fast-paced cardinal sign. Her cause of death was ruled as an accidental drowning with co-factors of heart disease (Sun) exacerbated by drug use (South Node square Lot of Nemesis). She died at 3:55 pm on February 11, 2012. The news spread like wildfire on Twitter, with a record-breaking 2.5 million tweets within an hour. This phenomenon is aptly described by her Moon and Jupiter in fiery Aries in opposition to her Lot of Nemesis. The Moon is the general significator of the public, and Jupiter expands whatever it touches.

The Place of Accomplishment

The Place of Accomplishment is the eleventh sign from the Lot of Fortune. It shows the means and ways that outcomes and benefits from the Lot of Fortune will manifest. Planets that occupy this eleventh place, or an aspect from the planet that rules the 11th place to the Lot of Fortune, can be very beneficial.

Jimmy Fallon's chart is a good example of the Place of Accomplishment. (See chart page 120) His Lot of Fortune is at 3° Taurus. The Place of Accomplishment is eleven signs forward (or two signs back) in Pisces. Jimmy's Jupiter-Ascendant conjunction in Pisces sextiles the PF and shows that he gains benefits through his personality, generosity, his wide range of talents, and by being a genial and witty host. Jimmy moved up the comedy career ladder at a blistering pace. He did stand-up comedy tours after college, moved to Los Angeles, was briefly on *Spin City* in 1998, and was invited to audition for *Saturday Night Live*. He joined the cast for the 1998-1999 season and was a full cast member by the summer of 1999. Within ten years he became the host of NBC's *Late Night* show. He was earning $11 million a year by 2013. In 2014, he succeeded Jay Leno as the host of *The Tonight Show*. That's a remarkable accomplishment for a 40-year old comedian in the fiercely competitive comedy sector of the entertainment business. His chart is pure comedy gold.

Chapter 10 Draconic Charts and Other Portals

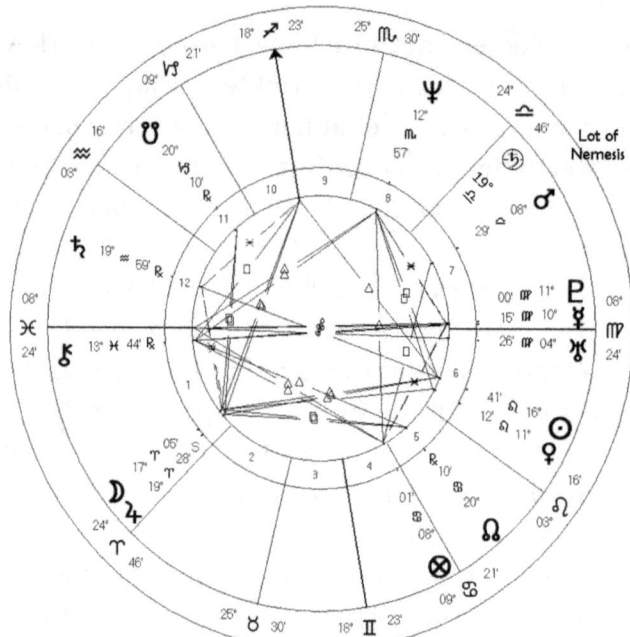

Whitney Houston
August 9, 1963, 8:55 pm EDT
Newark, New Jersey
Geocentric-Tropical
Placidus-True Node

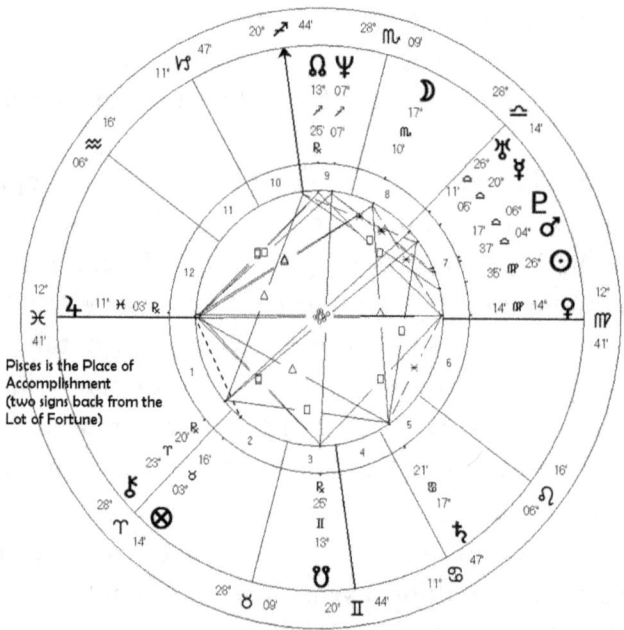

Jimmy Fallon
September 19, 1974, 6:22 pm EDT
Bay Ridge, NY
Geocentric-Tropical
Placidus-True Node

Chapter 11

Applied Astrology: Sample Charts

Seven charts have been selected to demonstrate the principles set forth in previous chapters. The chart delineations include elements of personal histories to give a context for how facets of fate, fortune, providence and destiny manifested for the individual. References to the relevant chapters or pages are provided in the chart descriptions.

Syd Barrett

Roger Keith "Syd" Barrett was born on January 6, 1946, in Cambridge, England (no time of birth, sunrise chart).[1] His chart demonstrates many of the fate markers described in previous chapters.

His chart is overloaded with natal planet-star contacts: Sun—Vega, Mercury—Aculeus, Venus—Facies, Mars—Procyon, Jupiter—Arcturus, Saturn—Pollux, Uranus—Rigel, Neptune—Diadem, North Node—Betelgeuse/Polaris, South Node—Acumen. It is very rare to see so many prominent planet-star contacts in a chart. It was a mixed blessing for Syd.

Syd Barrett, 1969
By Mick Rock
(permission requested)

Vega is the heliacal rising star. **Sun-Vega** describes a noted musician and artist, and Barrett's life themes resonate to the star's mythic origins. Vega is the alpha star of the constellation Lyra, the lyre. On Hermes's (Mercury's) first day of life, he stole Apollo's cattle by making them walk backwards in their own hoof-prints. It's an allegorical Greek myth explaining why the Sun's herd (ie, the planets) move in retrograde motion. Zeus/Jupiter made Hermes return the the cattle to Apollo. As an added apology, Hermes fashioned a seven-stringed lyre from a tortoiseshell and presented it to Apollo. The strings represent the planets.

Apollo, the Sun god, taught Orpheus how to play. According to legends, Orpheus could charm the birds from the sky, and one imagines he must have been very

Syd—Feb 1967 promo photo
(no copyright found)**

handsome, too. Barrett was a charming, witty, and a mischievous Puck character in the London clubs, wearing peacock ensembles of colorful velvet pants, paisley vests and ruffled poet's shirts. This was the iconic vagabond-aristocratic flower child look of the psychedelic movement. Barrett's overgrown, wildly tossed black hair accented his violet eyes, and he was quite the charismatic babe magnet. Syd associated with several different women friends of greater and lesser influence. Lindsay Korner is credited with outfitting him in hippie garb.

Orpheus is one of the few mythic characters who made a journey to the Underworld. After Orpheus was killed by wild women, Apollo placed his lyre in the northern heavens as a constellation. Vega is the most desirable North Star. The Sun, Mercury, and Jupiter are linked in the story of the heavenly lyre. Barrett was the *poète maudit* of the British psychedelic movement, and the pattern of his career is quite similar to that of Arthur Rimbaud, who wrote poetry for only three years. Those years, fueled with clouds of hashish over a pond of absinthe, rocked Paul Verlaine and the world of French symbolist poetry on its axis. Having completed his poetic savagery, Rimbaud disappeared into obscurity.*

Syd's chart features Jupiter/Arcturus in Libra sextile Mercury-South Node/Acumen-Aculeus at the Capricorn Gate, a dangerous portal to the Underworld and to immortality. Aculeus and Acumens are stars in the Scorpion's stinger that portend dangers and pitfalls. It's the abode of the Scorpion goddess Ishara-tam-tim, guardian of the entrance to Paradise, the Galactic Center. The multi-cultural myths about this zodiacal portal feature psycho-killer goddesses, poisons, and horrors. Mercury in detriment and his buddy, the exalted the South Node, are walking right into the zodiac's little shop of horrors.

*Rimbaud's chart also features a Mercury-South Node conjunction in Scorpio entangled with the stars of Kentaurus. Furthermore, his Saturn-Rigel conjunction squares the Neptune-Achernar conjunction in Pisces; his chart has a unique link between the stars at the beginning and end of the river Eridanus. Rimbaud and Barrett share some other chart placements. (Chart data: Arthur Rimbaud, born October 20, 1854, 6:00 am, Charleville Mezi, France; RR: AA, from Astro Databank)]

**Extensive image source searches were done to ascertain creative commons status or copyright information for photographs taken after 1949. If copyrighted images have been used without permission, it is unintentional. Please contact the author.

The South Node has far more power than Mercury in this position, and it can possess Mercury's body in order to channel the divine heights and daemonic depths of stellar narrativium of this zodiacal zone. The North Node is conjunct Betelgeuze and Polaris, so the exalted Nodal axis straddles a powerful stellar axis. Betelgeuze gives success. Polaris gives the ability to navigate toward the future, but this tends to be of more benefit to others rather than to the native.

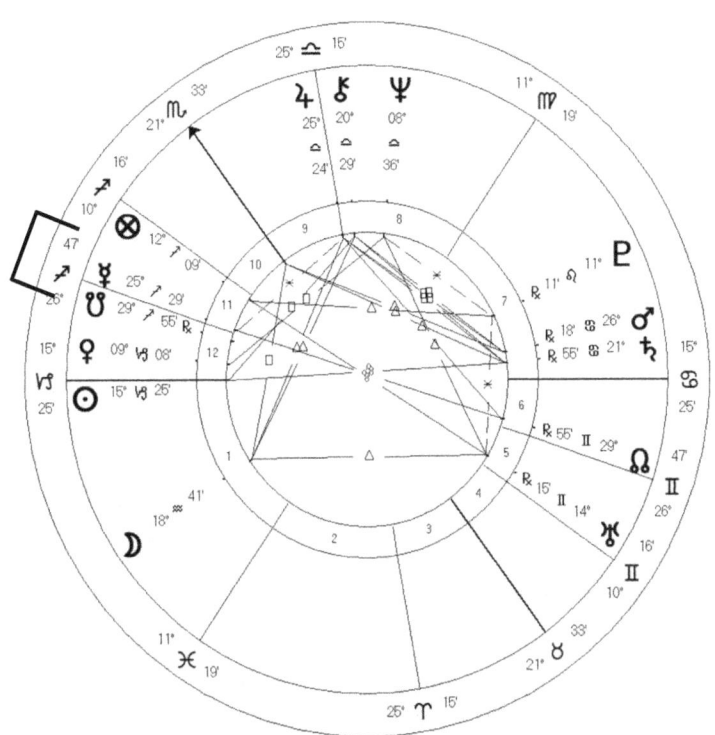

Syd Barrett
January 6, 1946, 8:14 am UT (Sunrise)
Cambridge, England
Geocentric-Tropical
Placidus-True Node

Uranus is conjunct Rigel as well as its own planetary north node. Rigel is in the maelstrom or whirlpool star-portal, Orion's foot in the river Eridanus. Syd was in one of the most exciting cities in the world, London, during the pop art, fashion, and rock n' roll explosion of the mid-1960s. This was the dominant British social and cultural vortex of the times.

Barrett was at the vanguard of the British psychedelic music trend as a founding member of Pink Floyd. The musicians started to connect in 1964 and began recording in 1965. During the summer of 1965, Barrett moved to Earlham. He took his first acid trip in a friend's garden. While under the influence of the drug, Syd placed an orange, a plum and a matchbox in a corner. He said it symbolized Venus and Jupiter. This imagery was used for the cover of **Syd Barrett**, a double album released in 1974. Syd read a great deal of mystical literature, including Grimm's Fairy Tales and the Wilhelm translation of the I-Ching. He became interested in a strange Sikh sect called Sant Mat. The cult's guru rejected him because he was too young. Syd's Mercury and South Node in Sagittarius have highly spiritual overtones with expansive sextiles to Jupiter and the Moon. Being rejected by the cult was a terrible blow, and he was intensely upset by it. Barrett's path in life might have been less destructive if he *had* found a spiritual home and some guidance at this critical juncture.

Syd wrote a great deal of the material on the band's first album **Piper at the Gates of Dawn**[2], released in 1967. The title is a quote from **The Wind in the Willows**.[3] His chart describes the album title, with the Nodes and Mercury at the Cancer and Capricorn Gates. Mercury invented shepherd's pipes made from reeds and is sometimes depicted playing this instrument.

Piper at the Gates of Dawn showcases Syd's eloquent and eclectic writing style. Songs like *Bike*, *Scarecrow* and *The Gnome* are reminiscent of nursery rhymes and fairy tales. It was described by rock music journalist Malcolm Dome as an album of a man "opening up his psychosis, opening up his psychology, opening up his disturbed yet quite brilliant mind."[4] Musician Robyn Hitchcock wrote "It was as if he was looking down on himself from somewhere else. There was a sort of detachment from...I guess his ego had got marooned twelve paces to the west of where Syd Roger actually was."[5] One song on the album is *Astronomy Domine*. The lyrics of the first verse are:

> Lime and limpid green, a second scene
> A fight between the blue you once knew.
> Floating down, the sound resounds
> Around the icy waters underground.
> Jupiter and Saturn, Oberon, Miranda
> And Titania, Neptune, Titan.
> Stars can frighten.

Syd's time as the north star of psychedelic rock was brilliant but brief. Padraig O'Connor wrote in his *Song of the Week* blog on July 29, 2013: "Rick Wright and Nick Mason believe that Syd Barrett's acid intake was the major cause of his breakdown. According to Rick, he changed fundamentally after one weekend. "He'd absolutely damaged himself beyond repair." He went from being a warm, outgoing charming character to a lost, confused soul. He'd lost the sparkle in his eyes. Syd was living with a community who believed in the Timothy Leary doctrine that you could become enlightened or "tuned in" with LSD. Rick claims that people were spiking Syd's tea with acid, and that he never would have intended to take so much of his own volition. Wright's opinion is that Syd took a huge overdose of acid. The schizophrenic tendencies were already there, but according to Gilmour, the acid acted as a catalyst for the decline in his mental health."[6]

Syd was no longer able to cope with the pressure to perform in public and produce new music. During the summer of 1967, Neptune in Scorpio squared his natal Moon, and Saturn in Aries squared his Capricorn Sun and Venus. Of focal interest, his Mercury and the South Node started thrashing when squared by Uranus in Virgo. These transits coincide with the purported "weekend overdose" that apparently took place during the late spring or summer of 1967, shortly before **Piper at the Gates of Dawn** was released. Syd's behavior became erratic, rude and unpredictable. He was dropped from the band in the spring of 1968 because he'd become too difficult to work with. He was hospitalized at the end of that year for psychiatric treatment for schizo-affective disorder.

Transiting Pluto in Virgo squared his Mercury-South Node as the decade ended. Syd made sputtering attempts to get back into the musical groove but failed. He became a total recluse in 1972 at the age of 26, as Saturn entered Gemini and opposed Neptune in Sagittarius. Peter Barnes, the band's manager, said "He's much bigger now as the silent cult-figure doing nothing than he was when he was functioning."[7] The dark romance of a beautiful young Englishman gone mad certainly increased his allure. "Barrett has been elevated into the position of becoming perhaps the leading mysterioso figure in the whole of rock ."[8]

Syd Barrett spent the rest of his life painting abstracts and gardening. Few of his paintings survive since it was his his habit to destroy them or paint over them after completion. Mercury-South Node in the Mula/Root nakshatra relates to creation/destruction. Abstract art is a deconstruction of images into shapes, colors and textures. Ideas are broken down into their raw components, much like Niritti breaks down the by-products of Shiva's dance of destruction so it can be digested and recycled by the cosmos.

Some of Syd's paintings are highly primitive. There's no title for this painting, so let's call it "Syd at the Gate." A man is being blown away by the Sun rising between two mountain

From http://www.sydbarrett.com/art.htm

peaks and glaring with an explosion of violent red beams. He could be singing a tribute to the rising Sun because he's in a posture of prostration. There's a cloud of red, white, blue and green between the mountain-top and the man. Perhaps it is a cluster of confused communication between the man and the mountaintop. Notice that only half of the man's body is visible; the bottom half is cut-off behind the mountain. Like Rahu-Ketu, he is cut in half. From an astrological standpoint, the man sees or senses all of the information (narrativium) that the cosmos is sending his way. He tries to honor it, but he cannot process everything the cosmos has to say. His mind attempts to comprehend, but he lacks the means for digesting and processing it. Ultimately, it has to be re-absorbed by the mountain. What's even more interesting is that the man's head contains the same colors, red, blue, and green, that are in the cloud. There's an area of hot pink at the bottom of the man's head, and the artist's name "Syd" is printed in this same pink. This color isn't used anywhere else in the image. The signals from the cosmos have saturated all but this small part of his being, and an isolated island in the back of his head still remains "Syd."

Syd's other occupation was gardening. The natural annual process of germination, growth, flowering, and deterioration reflect the seasonal cycles of Earth. Keeping his hands in the soil and retaining a close connection to these cycles was probably very soothing and stabilizing for his shattered psyche. It was a way for him to participate in life and give meaning to his existence, since the blooming of flowers is how God tells time. Mercury's ruler, Jupiter, is in Libra, the sign of beauty. Flowers are nature's most extreme and erotic form of natural beauty. His Aquarius Moon trines Jupiter, and his garden was his sustainable community of beauty. Growing plants, like having pets, is a source of joy, uncomplaining companionship, and unconditional love. Flowers demand only good soil and sufficient water. Gardening is a pastime and skill that sometimes appears in people whose charts feature planets at the Cancer and Capricorn Gates. The life cycle of plants is a featured component of the Persephone-Demeter-Hades myth.

Barrett's influence was so striking that his legend has stubbornly endured. His former band mates went out of their way to make sure that he continued to receive royalties. The Pink Floyd album *Wish You Were Here* is a tribute to him, especially the song "Shine On You Crazy Diamond": *Now there's a look in your eyes/ Like black holes in the sky...Come on you raver, you seer of visions/Come on you painter, you piper, you prisoner, and shine.* Syd's journey into the underworld, the depths of his own psyche, granted him the blessing (or curse) of immortality. Even in seclusion he was pestered by fans and the paparazzi. His health declined because of stomach ulcers and Type 2 diabetes, and he died of pancreatic cancer at the age of 60 on July 7, 2006.

Mercury in detriment (Sag) and conjunct the South Node and the stinger stars suggest a vulnerable, fragile mentality, but also the potential to be infused with divine inspiration. The sign's ruler, Jupiter, has a difficult square to Saturn and Mars in Cancer, both retrograde and particularly inimical in detriment and fall. The Aquarius Moon is in mutual reception with Saturn and receives Mars, and Syd was uncommonly sensitive to the pulse of the times. Mercury-South Node in the Scorpion's tail stars made it impossible for him to remain at the center of the Uranian vortex. The South Node augers the potential downfall of excess. The allure was a heightened state of mind. LSD opens bizarre doors of perception that can be advantageous in moderation, but for Syd the excess was perilous and wrecked his inner balance. He peaked and burned out within six years. Syd Barrett's unique spirit has phenomenal sticking power in the often cruel and contemptuous music industry.

Mercury the psychopompos carries the magic wand that allows entree into strange and forbidden realms. Syd carried Mercury's wand for a short period of time. His wand was an electric guitar, mirroring the lyre Mercury made for Apollo. One of his band mates even said that at times his playing was like magic. The magic led to forbidden realms that were too potent or alien for his senses. His life story parallels the myth of Orpheus—the enchanted musician whose magical playing helped the Argonauts sail safely past Circe's island, who lost his lover, and was torn apart by maenads. Maenads are the ancient equivalent of the pestering fans and paparazzi who hounded him until his death.

Syd performed his greatest musical feats as a young man and then virtually disappeared. Barrett's Mercury and South Node occupy a sign that is half man and half horse, and the LSD he consumed expanded his creativity but destroyed his mental and physical health. Thanks to his band-mates, Syd accumulated great wealth, as his siblings inherited £1.7 million at his death. After his personal belongings were sorted, a feverish auction netted £121,000 that was donated as a grants fund for art students.

Dane Rudhyar

Dane Ruhdyar was born Daniel Chenneviere on March 23, 1895, 12:42 am LMT, Paris, France. His chart is a potent demonstration of soul purpose indicators at work. The Moon, Mercury, and the North Node are all spearchuckers for the exalted Sun. They gave Rudhyar immense creative vitality and overflowing talents as an astrologer, author, composer, poet, and visionary philosopher. These doryphories are far enough ahead of the Sun that he was aware that *what he did* was not *who he was*. He was able to separate his abilities from his identity to an unusual extent.

Rudhyar changed the course of 20th century astrology by steering it toward a focus on soul purpose.[9] His skill sets were ninth house-related abilities. In ancient astrology, a natal combination of a powerful Mercury, Saturn, and ninth house factors signify an astrologer or priest. He's got this in spades with Mercury ruled by, and in mutual reception with, Jupiter and applying to trine Saturn, along with a Mercury-ruled 9th house and South Node. Rudhyar's spiritual approach and multi-disciplinary synthesis of concepts established the new paradigm of Humanistic Astrology. The Moon's sextile to Venus with Mirach, a talent star, and trine to Jupiter with Bellatrix, a success star, signifies his vastly prolific output, which included hundreds of articles, pamphlets, and books about astrology in addition to musical compositions, poetry, and philosophical works.

Mercury is associated with child prodigies. Rudhyar graduated from the Sorbonne with a degree in philosophy in his teens. He took the radical step of abandoning his family, name and culture when he relocated to the United States at age twenty-one. The name Rudhyar is derived from an avatar of Shiva called Rudra, a lightning god that is both a destroyer and regenerator. The name he chose signaled his intent!

Rudhyar had an unusually acute sense of purpose and destiny. This is shown by Mars-Neptune on the DSC and trine his MC. Mercury is conjunct Deneb Adige (alpha Cygnus) a star that gives great personal will power and the propensity for notable achievements and publication. He was born shortly before a solar eclipse. This gave him the impetus and will-fullness to abandon his name and family connections and create a new identity that reflected his self-determined purpose in the world. The potent Gemini stellium includes his 4th house ruler Mars surrounded by Neptune and Pluto. The antiscion of Pluto makes a partile trine to Rudhyar's North Node. Much like Jim Morrison and Jimmy Page, with Pluto-North Node conjunctions, Rudhyar plowed a new road in his field. Mars'

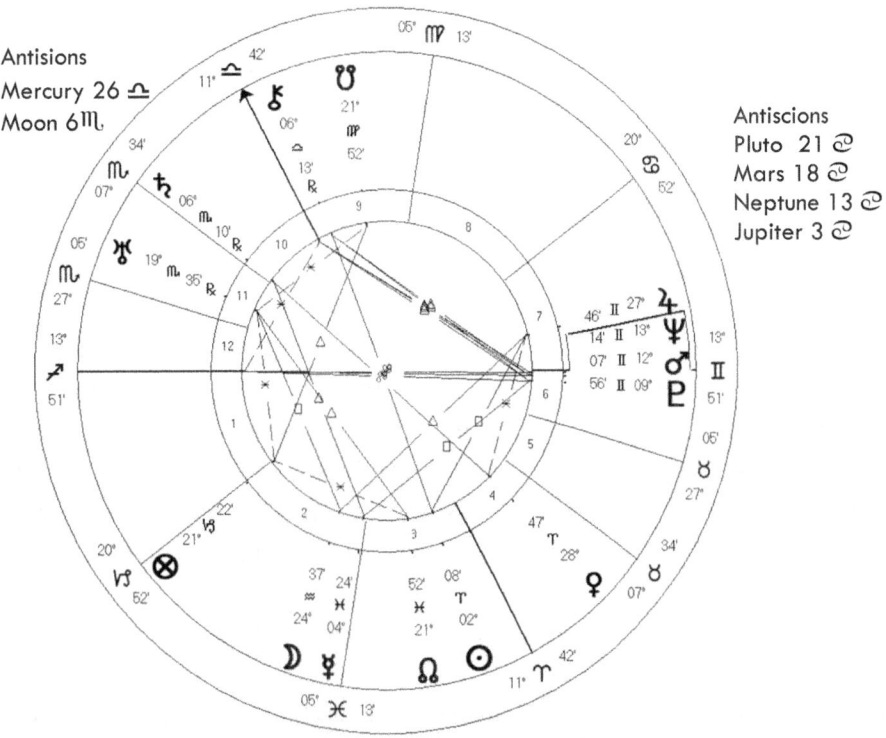

Dane Rudhyar
March 23, 1895, 12:42 am LMT
Paris, France
Geocentric-Tropical
Placidus-True Node

Dane Rudhyar – Soul Purpose Indicators

PLANET	SIGN	HOUSE	LORD	CONDITION	ASPECTS
Sun	Aries	5th	Mars	Exalted	-
Mercury	Pisces	4th	Jupiter	Fall	Trine Saturn, MR Jupiter Conjunct Deneb Adige
Moon	Aquarius	3rd	Saturn	Peregrine	Trine Jupiter
North Node	Pisces	4th	Jupiter	(mutable)	
South Node	Virgo	10th	Mercury	(mutable)	
Ascendant	13 Sag		Jupiter		
Heliacal Rising Star	(38 North)	Hamal (α Aries)			

antiscion trines Uranus, indicating exceptional originality and conceptual breakthroughs. Uranus occupies the Place of Accomplishment, the 11th place from the Lot of Fortune, and it sextiles the Lot. His accomplishments were groundbreaking. His Mercury and Moon antiscions form trines: Mercury's antiscion trines the Moon, and the Moon's antiscion trines Mercury. The potency of his spearchuckers is doubled. When he spoke, people listened.

Rudhyar explored and developed new astrological concepts over a fifty-year career by integrating holistic principles, Theosophy, Jungian depth-psychology, and Einsteinian physics. His core concepts included the idea that "...we are born with a purpose, to answer a fundamental need of the greater whole...to actualize our innate potentials which are contained in seed form at birth...".[10] He regarded astrology as a symbolic language. With Chiron trine Pluto, Rudhyar was able to "translate" concepts about the soul's evolution and purpose and share them with other astrologers. Chiron is in the 9th house, and he was a prophet who flourished in a foreign country, and a high priest of the human soul.

Rudhyar expanded into a transpersonal and galactic viewpoint toward the end of his life. The individual was a *transforming agent* whose efforts toward creating an integrated personality could lead to "freedom from the Collective and from unconscious, compulsive bondage to the values of one's culture..." This statement neatly encapsulates the possibility of yanking one's soul thread out of the Nodal candlewick. Perhaps he found this easier to do because his natal Uranus was trine/sextile his Nodal axis and conjunct Zuben Elschemali, a star that underscores intellectual precociousness and divergence from social conventions.

Rudhyar's natal planet-star contacts and antiscion aspects reveal an insistent theme of freedom and will power channeled through prolific creativity. His sophisticated expositions of astrological philosophy encompass the chief principles set forth in the descriptions of soul travel within the structure of the cosmos, as well as the inseparable bond between the soul and the whole. His natal indicators show quite clearly how he fulfilled his own soul's purpose by liberating his soul thread from the collective candlewick as a young man and consciously choosing a self-directed path of creative expression.

Audie Murphy: Two Charts Make Twice the Man
Audie Murphy was a noted military hero who had a subsequent career as a film actor.[11] His grave at Arlington Cemetery is the second-most visited site after JFK's grave. His singular actions on the battlefield are legendary. Audie was the most-decorated soldier of WWII, both for valor and wounds sustained in battle. In 2023, Gary Noel discovered Murphy's birth certificate in Texas and got his time of birth, changing the chart astrologers have used for decades.[12]

Childhood
Audie's childhood was just plain hard. He was born into a family with a dozen kids. His dad, a Texas sharecropper, abandoned the family during the Depression. Audie quit school in the 5th grade and got odd jobs to support the family. His mom died when he was fourteen-years old. Audie did exactly what Annie Oakley did—he learned how to hunt small game to supplement the family's food supplies, gaining speed and accuracy with a gun out of grim necessity.

Audie was sixteen when the Japanese bombed Pearl Harbor on December 7, 1941. He tried to join the Marines but was rejected. He was too young and too small, only 5' 5" and 110 pounds. He applied to the Army and Navy and was rejected by those branches as well. Then he made a life-altering decision that was a complete game-changer.

Audie's Birth Chart
Audie Murphy was born on June 20, 1925 at 8:00 pm CST, Kingston, Texas (see chart on page 132). His 4th quarter Gemini Moon was approaching the Sun at 29° Gemini 20', reaching its new phase at 12:27 am on June 21. Mercury at 0° Cancer was combust the Sun. That combination should send red flags up and dark shivers down the spine of any red-blooded astrologer. This was no 'piper at the gates' longing for a spiritual home in the mystical, mythical past; it was a berserker soul kicking and banging on the Cancer Gate and demanding admittance.

The change from 7:00 pm to the corrected 8:00 pm time of birth shifts the Ascendant from 21° Sagittarius to 5° Capricorn. The Sun, Moon and Mercury sink beneath the horizon to arrive at the New Moon just past midnight near the IC. It's a process-in-motion that marks the span of his life—from birth to death—in secondary progressions of the ASC/MC axis. Since he was born at the New Moon, the Ascendant is lovingly sandwiched between the Lots of Fortune and Spirit. Intense Sun-Moon-Mercury action on the Ascendant-Descendant axis creates a state of primal tension and the potential for big drama.

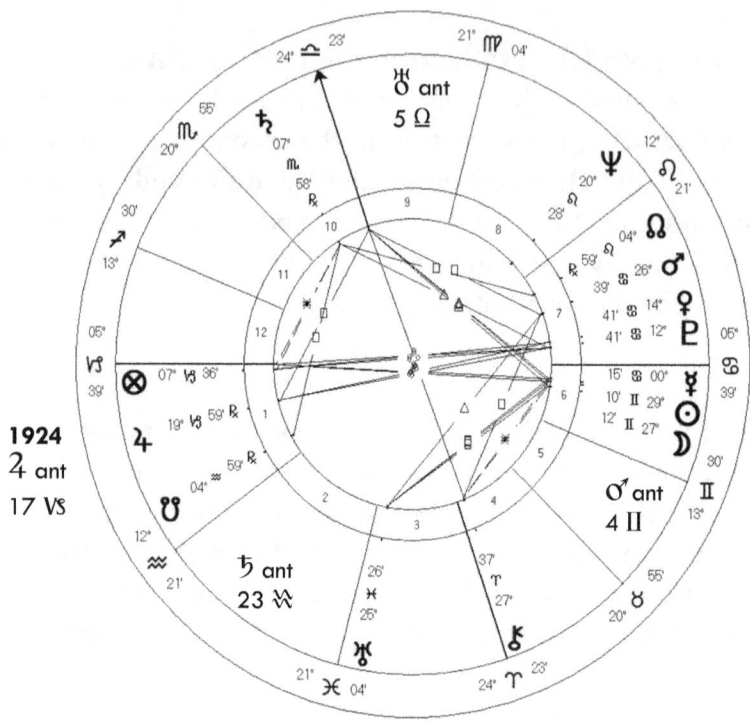

Audie Murphy
June 20, 1925, 8:00 pm CST
Kingston, Texas
Geocentric-Tropical
Placidus-True Node

His Ascendant ruler is Saturn. Audie's early life is a Saturnian sack-of-woe. He was beset by losses and limitations. The 8:00 pm chart places Saturn in Scorpio in the 10th house with Jupiter in Capricorn rising to the Ascendant. Mars in fall is angular and square Chiron at the IC. While Saturn is a grim taskmaster, in Audie's chart Saturn is closely sextile the Ascendant. Mars receives Saturn by sign and Saturn similarly receives Jupiter. This guy had to learn on his feet from an early age, take responsibility, and acquire a do-or-die attitude. Having a chart with the three superior planets well-configured and angular is quite powerful, even though the planets occupy signs that aren't comfortable or easy.

The outstanding aspect of the chart is Mars in Cancer trine Uranus in Pisces. This combination gives the juice to kick down doors and take names. The Sun, Moon and Mercury square Uranus, too. Audie had to break free of his childhood conditions. Mercury rules the 9th, while Mars rules the 4th house and squares the IC, indicating that he would fare better if he moved to a distant location. Curiouser and curiouser, Mars' antiscion at 4° Gemini trines Uranus' antiscion at 5° Libra in the 9th house, underscoring a change of fortune in foreign countries.

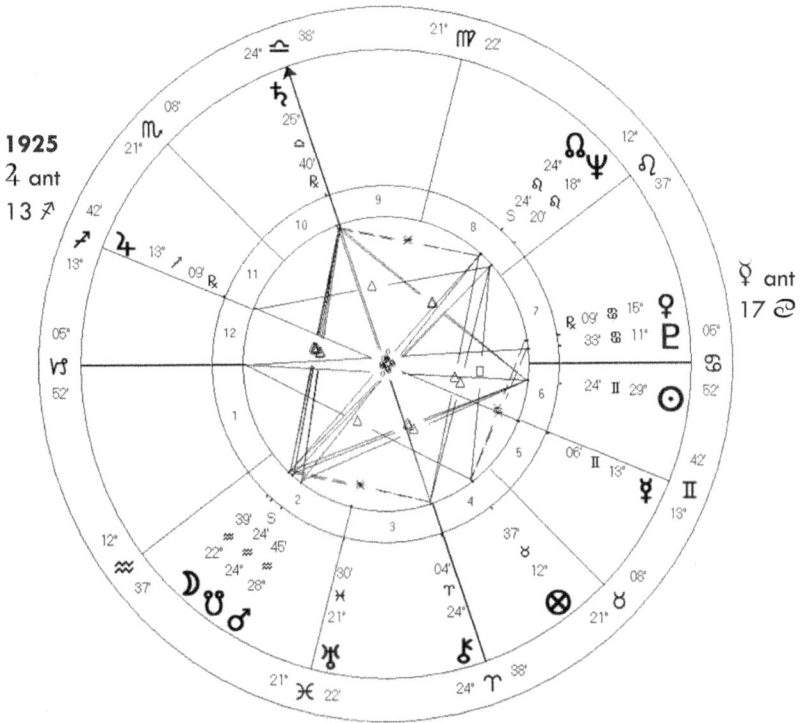

Audie Murphy - Falsified Birthdate
June 20, 1924, 8:00 pm CST
Kingston, Texas
Geocentric-Tropical
Placidus-True Node

This hidden antiscion trine is the secret key to Audie's phenomenal success, as will be shown below.

Bolstering this potential, Saturn's antiscion at 23° Aquarius trines his Libra Midheaven, giving him great potential as a leader with the gritty determination to succeed, rock-tough endurance and a high tolerance for pain. Saturn-ruled Jupiter gives access to that improved placement—Audie got smarter. He learned and traveled, took the hardest road, survived and overcame it. And he didn't just overcome it, he took on the rigors of war for two years and came back swinging every time, apropos of a boisterous Jupiterian drama. His deeds were nothing less than swashbuckling. Jupiter rising in Capricorn supplemented by a strong Saturn makes the impossible seem possible, and makes light of the most gruesome hardships.

Enlistment

The astrological detective now follows Audie into the Army. After being rejected, Audie got his older sister to write an affidavit saying he was born in 1924. This falsified birthday made him 18 years old in 1942, of age to serve. He ate more and gained a few pounds. This ploy worked and Audie was in the Army.

The fake 1924 birth chart is Audie's secret sauce (*see chart, page 133*). It's spectacular! The Moon and Mars sandwich the South Node in Aquarius in opposition to Neptune and the North Node. This spits bullets through the fog of war and the cameras aren't too far away. The opposition is part of a set of configurations – a Grand Trine in Air links the Moon and Sun to exalted 1st house ruler Saturn on the Midheaven. A Saturn-Chiron opposition dominates the cardinal Midheaven axis. The Venus-Pluto conjunction in his natal chart is repeated, as is the Sun's degree and position below the horizon.

In the 1924 chart, Mercury is free of the beams, eastern and strong in rulership. The tight opposition to Jupiter in Sagittarius sprinkles hot sauce on the astrological enchilada. Small but feisty, the little guy from Texas took on the Nazi war machine in ever-popular David versus Goliath fashion, gushing narrativium from the soles of his Army boots. With that hot South Node sandwich expressed through Saturn, the guy with this chart can be a super-soldier and become the king of the hill. No good myth ends with a dead hero: Audie had an angel on his shoulder with Jupiter on the 12th house cusp.

But this wasn't Audie's actual chart. *Or was it?* (cue creepy Hammer film segue music)

The Sun and Mercury in his actual 1925 chart flank the Cancer Gate at 29° Gemini and 0° Cancer—the spongiest, most permeable spot in the zodiac and a primary soul portal. Many prison escapes occur with planets at that spot. It is a gate between states of being. Audie changed his "being" by giving the Army a different date of birth and was able to slip past the age barrier.

A brief diversion here: many years ago I read an article by Linda Johnsen in *The Mountain Astrologer*.* She wrote about an ancient Vedic astrologer who would meditate on an elected birth chart and wear it like a mantle in order to manifest a particular goal. Before you start rubbing your knuckles, Ms. Johnsen wrote that this is a very dangerous practice. With a bit of thought, it's easy to see why that would be true. In this wildly unusual case of astrological legerdemain, Audie, a child of necessity, assumed the mantle of another birth chart to achieve his goal.

*Apologies, I wasn't able to track down the title and date of this article, but am fairly certain it was published in the late 1990s.

His real birth chart is connected to the false 1924 chart. The Sun is, of course, at the same degree. The 1924 chart features Mercury's antiscion at 17° Cancer conjunct Venus-Pluto in both charts. Audie assumed the role of the embattled hero in a do-or-die Plutonian conflict. The 1925 Moon-South Node-Mars stellium conjunct his natal Saturn antiscion at 23° Aquarius is a spectacular guts-and-glory combination. The 1924 Saturn conjuncts both Midheavens and squares the 1925 Mars. The secret sauce is that the 1924 and 1925 Jupiters swap antiscion "ninja" conjunctions (13° Sagittarius = 17° Capricorn; 19° Capricorn = 11° Sagittarius).

Audie manifested both charts simultaneously. From 1943 until 1945, Neptune occupied the early degrees of Libra and activated Audie's natal Mars-Uranus antiscion trine. By 1945, Chiron joined Neptune in Libra. The invasion of Normandy took place in June 1944 and by early 1945, the Germans were on the run but hadn't yet been defeated. The liberated French re-constituted their army and chased a German battalion to the Ill River in a region called the Colmar Pocket. The US 3rd Infantry division was sent to reinforce French troops. As if being in a war wasn't bad enough, the winter of 1945 was extremely cold and the weather conditions were brutal.

First Lieutenant Audie Murphy and Company B were attacked on the outskirts of Holtzwihr, France by six tanks and around 250 German infantrymen on the frigid morning of January 26, 1945. All of the officers were killed and 102 of the 120 enlisted men were killed or wounded. Murphy ordered the survivors to fall back into the woods while he covered their retreat. He spotted a .50-caliber machine gun on the turret of a burning tank destroyer. Knowing the position had to be held at all costs, Murphy climbed onto the turret and fired the machine gun at the oncoming Germans while requesting artillery fire over the radio. When asked how far away the Germans were, he replied "If you just hold the phone a minute, I'll let you talk to one of the bastards."[13] Murphy's deadly fire forced the German tanks to retreat to the tree line. Murphy's recollection was "...for the first time in three days my feet were warm." He made his one-hour one-

Audie Murphy firing the machine gun on a burning tank. *To Hell and Back*, 1952. Universal

man stand with US artillery shells landing very nearby. The billowing smoke from the burning tank and bombs obscured his position so the Germans couldn't determine the source of the deadly bullet-fire.

As the Germans fell back, Murphy's field phone went dead. Exhausted and bleeding, he climbed off of the burning tank and limped back into the forest. The tank blew up a few minutes later. He returned to his company and helped organize a counterattack, dislodging the Germans from the whole area. Thanks to Lt. Murphy, the Army captured Holtzwihr on January 27 and Germans removed their men and materiel from the area.

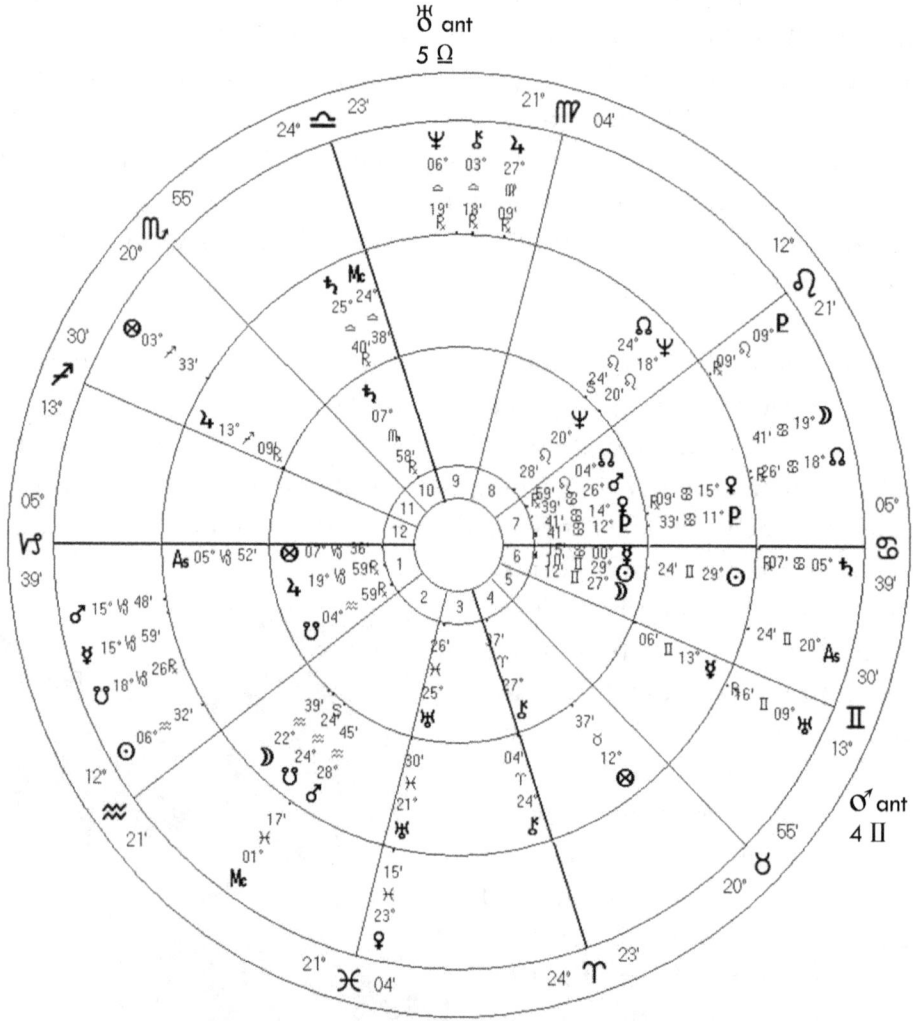

Audie Murphy 1924 and 1925 at the Battle of Riedwihr
Inner Wheel: June 20, 1925, 8:00 pm CST, Kingston, TX
Middle Wheel: June 20, 1924, 8:00 pm CST, Kingston, TX
Outer Wheel: Transits for January 26, 1945, 2:15 pm, Colmar, France
Geocentric-Tropical-Placidus-True Node

The transits during Audie's stand at Ridhwihr make powerful connections to his 1924 and 1925 charts. A transiting Mercury-Mars conjunction in Capricorn opposed the transiting Moon conjunct his Venuses. The transiting South Node was draped like a troop of angels around his natal Jupiter, protecting him from being burned or critically injured in the tank, and delaying the tank's explosion until he was out of range. The transiting Aquarius Sun activated a Grand Trine with transiting Neptune and Chiron (leg wounds) and his natal Mars-Uranus antiscion trine in air signs.

Audie Murphy manifested the greatest strengths of *both* charts. The skills gained in his hard-scrabble youth turned him into a star performer on the battlefield. The little soldier who kept beating the bad guys earned a legendary position in the American mythos.

Post War Career
Audie was sent to the infirmary to recover, received another Medal of Honor to add to his 20 other awards for valor, and arrived back in Texas just in time for his twentieth birthday. He transferred from the US Army to the US Army National Guard and helped train other soldiers. The US Army freely used his name and image for promotions – he was their golden boy, the most decorated soldier of the war.

In 1948, actor Jimmy Cagney saw Audie's face on a magazine cover. He tracked him down to extend an opportunity to come to Hollywood and get into film work. Audie spent a year training with drama and voice coaches but was slow to get acting jobs. Eventually he got roles in ensemble cast films and then leading roles in genre B-movies, mostly Westerns and crime thrillers. His writer friend David McClure helped him get a writing contract in 1947, and the book *To Hell and Back* was published by Henry Holt and Company on February 28, 1949. Once again, both 1924 and 1925 charts are activated by an Aquarius Moon-Venus, transiting Neptune square his Pluto, and a handy Jupiter return to Capricorn.

Lt. Audie Murphy receives the French Legion of Honor and the Croix De Guerre with palms from General De Lattre de Tassigny in the Invalides, Paris, July 16, 1948. AP

The book was a bestseller. Universal-International picked up the film rights a few years later. It was a good deal for

Audie—he received $25,000 for the rights, a $100,000 acting fee, plus 10% of the film's net profits. His performance was praised. **To Hell and Back** (1955) was one of the most realistic war films of the 1950s. Murphy received an estimated $1 million in royalties.

Lt. Audie Murphy with medals.
Wiki Commons

Portraying himself in a film had emotional costs. In an interview, Murphy tried to explain the "strange jerking back and forth between make-believe and reality" that filming the role evoked in him, "between fighting for your life and the discovery that it's only a game and you have to do a retake because a tourist's dog ran across the field in the middle of the battle."[14] He tried to launch a sequel called **The Way Back** but couldn't get a script good enough to attract studio financing.

Just as his star reached its height, the cinematic studio system broke down. Actors had to contract for their own roles. Transiting Neptune shifted from a square to his Venus, to a square to his Jupiter. The burgeoning television industry offered an alternative. He took guest roles in TV westerns and talk shows. Audie was the lead in the short-lived 1961 TV series *Whispering Smith*. He had far fewer film roles during the 1960s. His final film, **A Time for Dying**, was a 1969 Western.

After his return from Europe, Audie suffered badly from PTSD, experiencing insomnia, bad dreams, wild mood swings, and other symptoms. He was one of the first soldiers to speak about it openly and encouraged other soldiers to get help. He described his post-war experience in 1962: "War robs you mentally and physically, it drains you. Things don't thrill you anymore. It's a struggle every day to find something interesting to do."[15] When he realized he had become addicted to Placidyl, a potent sleeping pill, he locked himself in a motel room for a week and went cold turkey.

The transits of Saturn and Uranus took their toll. Uranus moved into his 6th house and made conjunctions to his Sun, Moon and Mercury by the mid-1950s. Audie's mental health and sleep cycles were disrupted. Saturn transited his Libra Midheaven in 1952 and 1953. Although it's mindboggling to consider, Audie didn't have his first Saturn return until the late 1950s. He was an incredibly young hero, at 18 to 20-years old during his military service in Europe from 1943-1945.

Sudden bursts of explosive temper ruined his first marriage to actress Wanda Hendrix within two years. He then married former flight attendant Pamela Archer and had two sons with her in a long-term marriage. In addition to his film work, Audie owned two ranches and bred quarter horses. Horse racing resulted in a bad gambling habit, leaving his finances in a poor state. In 1968, he struggled with the IRS over unpaid taxes, and made it worse by getting caught in a bogus Algerian oil deal and losing $260,000. Saturn in Aries squared his Venus-Pluto conjunction, Neptune squared its natal position, and the South Node crossed over his dominant Saturn. What he had gained was mostly lost. In May 1970 he was arrested in Burbank and charged with battery and assault with intent to commit murder in a dispute with a dog trainer. He was later acquitted in court.

> "A fugitive from the law of averages"

Audie struggled to repair his fortunes. He was offered a chance to participate in a business that built pre-fab houses. He and five others took a private plane to Roanoke, Virginia on May 28, 1971. Mars in Aquarius squared his natal Saturn. The airplane was caught in a dense fog and low-lying clouds and the plane crashed into the side of a mountain at 12:08 pm. All passengers were killed. A retrograde Jupiter-Neptune conjunction was sextile Pluto at 27° Virgo, forming a Yod with Audie's natal Chiron. There were several quincunxes in Audie's chart at his time of death, leading one to suspect that he had many different situations tugging at him, and may not have wanted to take the trip that day.

When Walter Cronkite announced the death of Audie Murphy on May 31, 1971, he said that Murphy was "a fugitive from the law of averages."[16] Manifesting two charts at the same time had much to do with improving his odds of survival. Like many youthful prodigies, becoming the most decorated soldier of World War 2 by age 20 created a peak experience he couldn't replicate or match as he got older. Nevertheless, Lieutenant Audie Murphy is an example of real courage and an American hero. His story deserves to be remembered and shared.

Amalie "Emmy" Noether

Emmy Noether was a German mathematician who made significant contributions to abstract algebra during the first part of the 20th century.[17] Many notable mathematicians regard her as the most important woman in the history of math.

She was born in Erlangen, Germany in 1882. Her father was a mathematician. Emmy was a smart and friendly girl, but she was near-sighted and had a minor lisp as a child. Emmy was the oldest child with three younger brothers who died in tragic circumstances. Emmy passed exams to teach French and English and qualified to teach at girls schools, but instead opted to study math at the University of Erlangen where her father was a professor. She passed her exams in 1903, completed her doctorate in 1907, and worked at the Mathematical Institute of Erlangen from 1908 to 1915 without pay, since women were excluded from academic positions.

Emmy Noether, circa 1905

Emmy was invited to join the mathematics department at the University of Göttingen in 1915, but after objections by other faculty members, she was forced to lecture under another (male) professor's name. Her paper *Invariante Variationsprobleme* was presented on July 26, 1918 at the Royal Society of Sciences at Gottingen by her colleague, Felix Klein. This paper demonstrates Noether's Theorem, "one of the most important mathematical theorems ever proved in guiding the development of modern physics, possibly on par with the Pythagorean theorem."[18] High praise, indeed!

Her job and position were approved in June 1919 and she became a Privatdozent, a title that indicates that she held degrees and was approved to teach. She continue to be unpaid for her work until 1923, when she finally became an untenured professor. During her years at the university, she was at the center of a hub of international mathematicians producing extraordinary work. She nurtured a group of young students called "Noether's boys" and supervised doctoral students, gaining the nickname of "dissertation-mother".

Emmy gave an address at the 1932 International Congress of Mathematicians in Zürich. This address is considered the high point of her career. Her mathematical skills received worldwide recognition. Emmy's work in abstract algebra is considered one of the most distinctive innovations of 20th century math.

Emmy's moment of glory was short-lived. The Nazis ousted Jews from university positions in 1933. She was offered and accepted a teaching position at Bryn Mawr College in Pennsylvania. She taught graduate and post-doctoral students. She also lectured and did research at the Institute for Advanced Study in Princeton, New Jersey.

Since Emmy worked for many years without being paid, her lifestyle was necessarily frugal. Even when she finally earned a decent salary, she chose to live simply. She saved half of her salary to bequeath to her nephew. Her focus on math was so intense that she ignored her appearance and manners. Students describe her speaking at lunch and spilling food on her dress, and wiping it off with a complete lack of concern. Her hair was sometimes in disarray during lectures. She didn't follow lessons plans and apparently ad-libbed her classroom discussions. Since she spoke quickly, not all students appreciated her style. Her contributions to in-person discussions could be very deep and subtle.

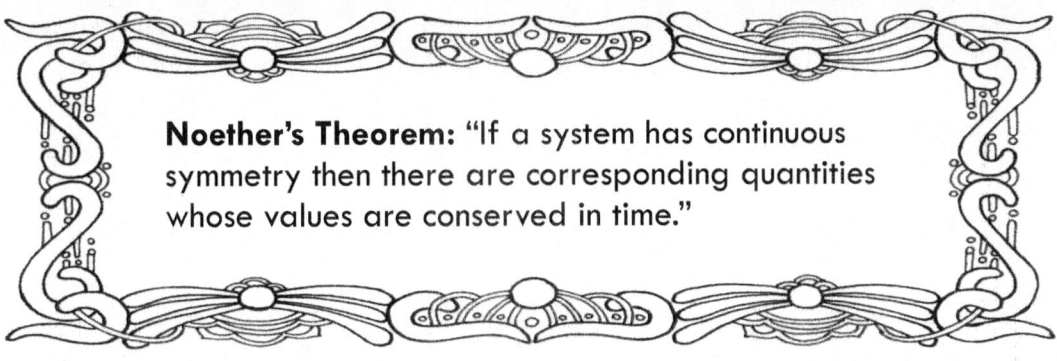

Noether's Theorem: "If a system has continuous symmetry then there are corresponding quantities whose values are conserved in time."

Emmy received the Ackermann-Teuner Memorial award with colleague Emil Artin in 1932. She was 50-years old. The monetary reward was £500, and it was seen as a long delayed acknowledgement of her work in the field. She was frustrated because she was never invited to become a member of the Academy of Sciences, nor was she ever promoted to a full professorship. When Jews were expelled from civil service positions in 1933, Emmy was calm and gave support to others. She created a new circle of four female students at Bryn Mawr who were called "the Noether girls." All of these women went on to have significant careers in mathematics.

A tumor was discovered in her pelvis in April 1935. During the operation, doctors discovered an ovarian cyst the size of a cantaloupe. She appeared to recover normally at first, but developed an extremely high fever and died on April 14. Tributes were written by mathematicians from around the world.

> "In the judgment of the most competent living mathematicians, Fräulein Noether was the most significant creative mathematical genius thus far produced

since the higher education of women began. In the realm of algebra, in which the most gifted mathematicians have been busy for centuries, she discovered methods which have proved of enormous importance in the development of the present-day younger generation of mathematicians."[19]

—Albert Einstein

Fellow algebraist Bartel van der Waerden said that her originality was "absolutely beyond comparison."[20]

Emmy Noether's birth chart is extraordinarily focused with a grand stellium in Taurus including Saturn, Neptune, Chiron, Jupiter and Pluto that mostly occupy the 8th house. The Moon and South Node are conjunct on Mirfak (alpha Perseus) and sextile her Aries Sun in the 6th house. Her interest was in her studies and students, and other matters were peripheral. The Moon's ruler and 9th house ruler Mercury seems a bit lonesome by itself in Pisces in the 5th house, but note that Mercury's antiscion is conjunct her Ascendant, which is conjunct Arcturus.

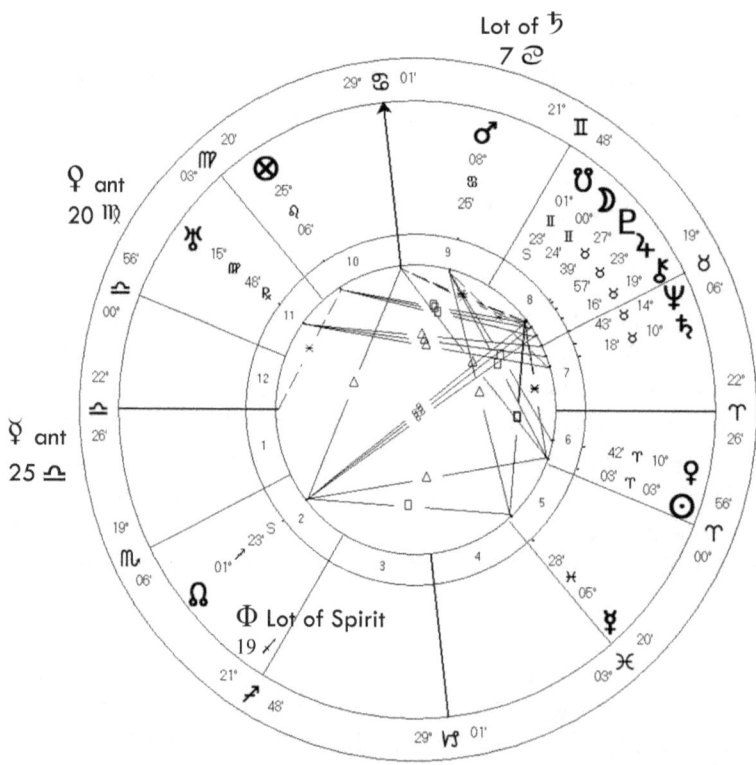

Emmy Noether
March 23, 1882, 8:00 pm LMT
Erlangen, Germany
Geocentric-Tropical
Placidus-True Node

A notable quality of Arcturus is the propensity for friendships. Mercury is conjunct Sadalachbia (gamma Aquarius) also with benefits from good friendships.

Generosity was a life-theme, as she shared her ideas and allowed other mathematicians to publish her work. She was known for being patient and helpful with students, although she demanded precision. In her obituary, Van der Waerden wrote "Completely unegotistical and free of vanity, she never claimed anything for herself, but promoted the works of her students above all."[21] Emmy's powerful Taurus stellium would seem to indicate a tendency toward possessiveness, but the sign's ruler Venus has its antiscion at 20° Virgo, forming trines to her Taurus planets. Natal Uranus also trines the Taurus stellium, so her values were unconventional. At a time when few women were able to get an advanced education, she achieved a doctorate. This, in part, was because of her father's job at Erlangen. Saturn rules the 4th house of the father. Uranus has a tight trine to Neptune, so one imagines her father Max was very proud of his unusual oldest child. He continued to financially support and encourage her to continue her studies. Venus' antiscion is close to Uranus, which is conjunct Asterion (beta Canes Veneticia), a star notable for promoting a desire to belong to a group.

Emmy's Hellenic Lots merit consideration. Her Lot of Fortune is in Leo in the 10th house and square Jupiter-Pluto. What she found in her environment were opportunities to plumb the depths of abstract mathematics and algebra. Jupiter and Pluto occupy the Gate of the Kosmocrator, the last decan of Taurus. It's a zone of intense concern around esoteric matters, the origin of life and the cosmos, and the fate of the soul after death. Jupiter is conjunct Caput Algol, a star linked to diamonds in astrological magic. Emmy's intellect was like a diamond cutting through the fabric of algebra to discover deeper layers and more nuanced expressions. Although in some ways she was "beheaded" by giving her ideas to other mathematicians, her generosity of spirit was such that the community revered and supported her, and appreciated her extraordinary capabilities. Pluto is conjunct the Pleiades, a star cluster purported to be the origin of human life on planet Earth. To follow her chart themes, the Pleiades are a group of siblings. Emmy's three brothers didn't fare well, and with ruler of the 3rd house Jupiter in the 8th house, her brothers died untimely.

The Moon and South Node occupy the Place of Accomplishment, the 11th sign from the Lot of Fortune. What Emmy accomplished in one respect is uniquely lunar—she was the "dissertations-mother" and her students were "Noether's boys" or "Noether's girls." Although Emmy never married or had children, she helped her students give birth to their greatest abilities through dedicated support and coaching. The Moon's application to the South Node's "ditch" is evident in the many years she worked without pay or an official job title because of her gender. Imagine working for fifteen years—not simply working but becoming one of the greatest practitioners in a field of study—and not receiving any type of remuneration for it. The men around her knew she was extraordinary, but no amount of pressure from her colleagues could abate the gender discrimination of the society in which she labored. Emmy *was* frustrated by this unconscionable insult to her abilities, but she apparently was able to put her feelings aside and focus on what she enjoyed most, the math and her students.

The Lot of Spirit (Sun) is at 19° Sagittarius. It has a connection to its dispositor Jupiter through a square to Venus' antiscion, which trines Jupiter. It's a bit second-hand. Since Emmy was born after sunset, her Lot of Spirit has less clout than the Lot of Fortune. It occupies her 2nd house, an area where she fared poorly for many years and had to survive on nothing. Her Lot of Saturn or Nemesis shows constraints and limitations. It's conjunct her Mars in Cancer, in fall and out-of-bounds at 25° North. Emmy was almost entirely surrounded by men in the rarified atmosphere of an academic university department. She was not invited to join academic societies and received no academic prizes until 1932. Since she was shunned, a colleague presented her paper in 1918. A planet in fall is ignored and appeals fall on deaf ears. Mars rules her 2nd, 6th, and 7th houses: she wasn't paid, she didn't have an official job title for many years, and she never married. Taurus endures! She held on long enough to get a salaried position and did better after she relocated to a foreign country (a 9th house matter). The Lot of Saturn indicates the quality of death. Her chart is very specific about this. The Lot of Nemesis and Mars square her Sun and Venus in Aries. She spiked an extremely high fever after having surgery (both Mars matters) on a uterine tumors and an ovarian cyst (Venus). Her end was swift and likely painless as she lapsed into a coma during her final hours—cardinal signs are speedy. She was only 53-years old.

Noether's work has been divided into three "epochs": 1908 to 1919, 1920 to 1926, and from 1926 to 1935. These periods are distinguished by the outer planets. Uranus was in Capricorn trine her Neptune in 1908. Uranus was in Pisces conjunct her Mercury in 1920, and at the end of Pisces and sextile her Jupiter-Pluto in 1926. Pluto was at 23° Cancer and sextile natal Jupiter when she died.

Ursula Le Guin

Ursula was born on October 21, 1929, just as the New York stock market was in the process of crashing. Her literary career spanned six decades and she's a noted author of science fiction and fantasy novels, poetry, literary criticism, translations, and children's books. [22]

Ursula's parents were well-educated. Her father Alfred Kroeber was an anthropologist and her mother Theodora had a graduate degree in psychology. She had three older brothers and the family had a large book collection. They had a summer home in Napa Valley and lived in Berkeley during the academic year. Ursula received her BA degree in Renaissance French and Italian literature from Radcliffe College in 1951 and was a member of Phi Beta Kappa honor society. She earned a MA in French at Columbia University in 1952, and won a Fulbright grant to continue studies in France. She met and married her husband Charles Le Guin in 1953. The marriage ended her quest for a doctorate. She taught French and worked as a secretary until she became a mother. Two daughters were born in 1957 and 1959. Charles and Ursula moved to Portland, Oregon, where their son was born in 1964. They remained in Portland for the rest of their lives.

Ursula began writing in the late 1950s, although she was constrained by childcare duties. Her literary efforts continued while she raised children and worked various jobs through the 1960s. Her early works were five novels set in the fictional country of Orsinia. They were rejected by publishers because the books were considered "inaccessible." She found a more receptive audience by writing short science fiction stories for magazines. She was ignored by critics. Her first novel was finally published in 1966. Her second and third novels received critical attention. Le Guin's favored literary theme features a protagonist compelled to take a journey that also becomes a journey of self-discovery, identity, a broadened mindset, and a reconciliation of opposing forces.

Ursula's Earthsea novels were published in 1968 and 1969. *The Left Hand of Darkness* explored gender themes and feminist issues. It won the Hugo and Nebula Awards for Best Novel. Ursula was the first woman to win these awards. These books are her masterpieces. Additional Earthsea books were published in 1971 and 1972. She won the Hugo Award again in 1973 for *The Word for World is Forest*, a book focused on colonialism and militarism. It was inspired by her anger over the Vietnam War. Her 1974 novel *The Dispossessed* won the Hugo and Nebula Awards, making her the first person to win both awards for two books.

Le Guin refocused on writing for younger audiences in the 1980s. She continued to write books in the fantasy worlds established in earlier novels, and kept winning awards into the 2000s.

Toward the end of her life, Le Guin shifted to non-fiction. Her work was strongly influenced by her father's interest in anthropology, multi-cultural mythology, sociology, philosophy, and Jungian archetypes. Her first Earthsea novel is credited with presenting the shadow archetype, although she hadn't read Jung's work before writing it. The fantasy world of Earthsea is sustained through a Taoist type of balance between the land and sea, the people and their environment, light and dark. Characters misunderstanding the need for balance is depicted as problematic rather than the good-versus-evil tropes in most books.

Ursula stood by her principles. She refused a Nebula Award in 1977 because an Eastern Bloc author was refused membership. The book being awarded was about political intolerance. She was attracted to Taoism and Buddhism and published a translation of the *Tao Te Ching* in 1997. Le Guin resigned from the Authors Guild in 2009 to protest its endorsement of Google's book digitization project, which involved significant copyright issues. Le Guin publicly chastised Amazon in 2014 during a speech at the National Book Awards over its excessive control over the publishing industry. Le Guin was also dragged into conflicts about how her books were assigned into genres. Her Earthsea novels were classified as "children's books," but they can be read by people of any age. She suggested the term "social science fiction" to distinguish books that focused on human conflicts rather than problems with purely scientific issues. Le Guin's novels feature leading characters with different skin colors, female, and androgynous protagonists. She was a pioneer in what is now categorized as feminist science fiction. She acknowledged her early tendency to cast male main characters and frame her stories in male-dominated societies dominated by heterosexual relationships. Le Guin made an effort to change her practices in this regard.

In addition to the journey-to-self-discovery theme, Le Guin's secondary theme was the coming-of-age story, where the central character's story culminates in a rite of passage. These central themes incorporate ideas about the proper and improper uses of power. Le Guin created imaginary alternative political systems and contrasting levels of social freedoms, including slavery.

The irony of being a notable writer is becoming a topic of critical discourse. Le Guin's works were so important, particularly through the 1970s, that she became a subject of academic interest and a focus for literary critics. Her books had ripple effects in radio, stage, television and cinema. In 2016, David Streitfeld described her as "America's greatest living science fiction writer"[23] Author Margaret Atwood praised Le Guin's "sane, smart, crafty and lyrical voice."[24] adding that social injustice was a powerful literary motivation in Le Guin's output.

Ursula Le Guin died at her home in Portland on January 22, 2018 at the age of 88. She had been ill for several months.

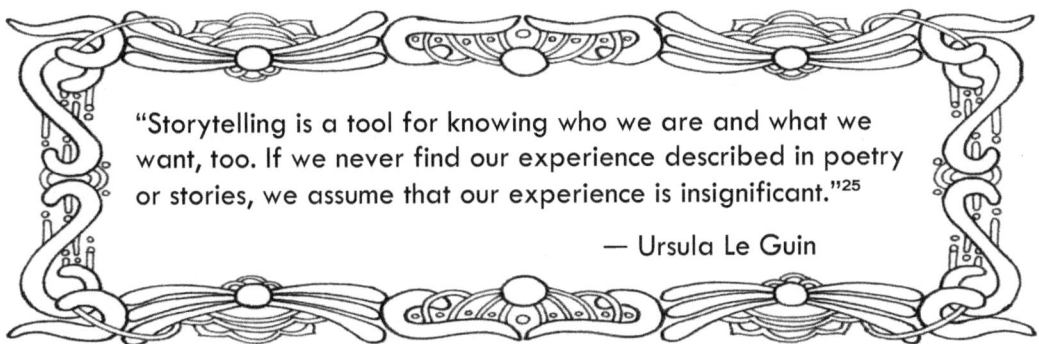

"Storytelling is a tool for knowing who we are and what we want, too. If we never find our experience described in poetry or stories, we assume that our experience is insignificant."[25]

— Ursula Le Guin

Ursula's Birth Chart

The above quote touches at the heart of astrology—understanding and validating the human experience. People are at the center of their own stories. Whether astrologers dig into myths or not, human lives do follow patterns and there are moments when those patterns can be changed.

The North Node and Chiron rise toward Ursula's Taurus ASC and trine her Lot of Fortune. The stuff of storytelling was something she was able to access in her home and daily environment. Her father studied the Yahi tribe and her mother wrote a biography about the last known member of the tribe. Ursula grew up in a home where tribal affiliations were visceral, especially the lack of a tribe. This resonates strongly with Chiron. Her early reading led her to myths and early science fiction stories. Mars is conjunct the South Node and has extra power by being in rulership, angular, and the sect malefic in good condition. Ursula could dig deeply into peoples' deepest motivations, fears, desires and longings and transfer that information into her fictional characters. The yoke from the past came in the form of male-dominated literature. She was surrounded by brothers reading fiction written by men featuring leading male characters. The burdens of the past that the South Node carries don't have to be a life-sentence, though. Le Guin broke free of male-centered novels and crafted novels featuring women or androgynous characters. Doing so helped her create a genre-within-a-genre. Mars is conjunct Crux, the alpha star of the Southern Cross. Its meanings include broadening of the mind and having a keen interest in spirituality.

Her chart ruler Venus is near Mercury in Libra in the 6th house. Her focus was on her work and her creative life. The planet that most closely aspects her ASC is Neptune in her 5th house. There must have been days when her head was in the clouds she spun stories about people on other worlds. Rearing small children must have been difficult. In a speech titled "Prospects for Women in Writing," given in Portland, Oregon in 1986, Le Guin said, "If you want your writing to be taken seriously, don't marry and have kids, and above all, don't die. But if you have to die, commit suicide. They [men] approve of that."[26] Ursula could be pithy! Mercury in opposition to Uranus signifies verbal zingers and snipes.

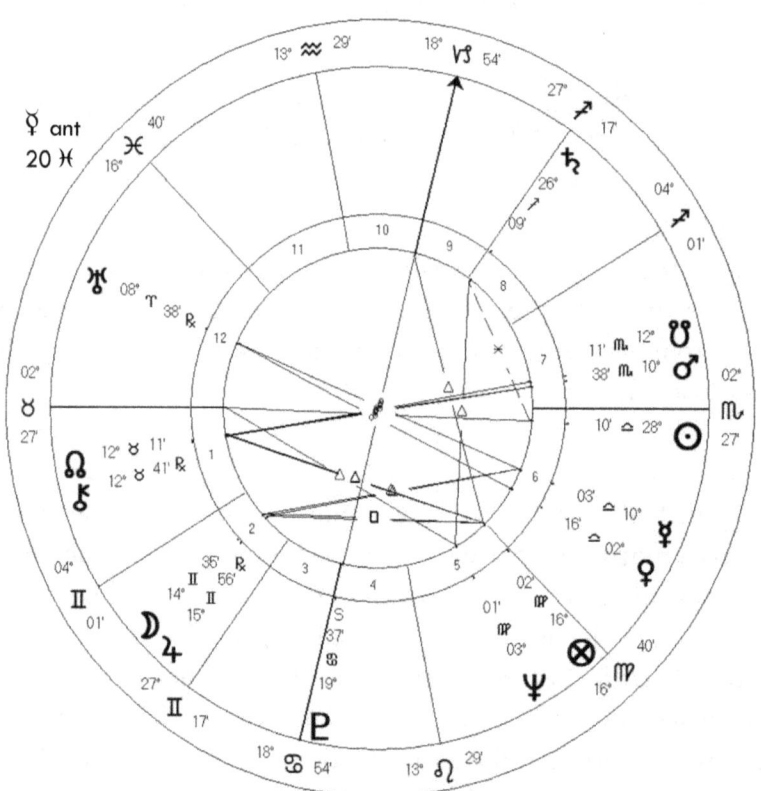

Ursula Le Guin
October 21, 1929, 5:31 pm PST
Berkeley, California
Geocentric-Tropical
Placidus-True Node

One of her strongest aspects is the sextile between the Sun and Saturn. Drive and discipline kept her going during the years before her efforts were accepted for publication, and discipline kept her at her craft for over six decades. Saturn produces legacies and opuses that live on after the creator passes. Saturn is conjunct the Galactic Center. Her fantasy-world novels from the 1960s and 1970s morphed into series with sequels added over many years. Her imaginary worlds had evolving casts of characters that faced different issues and challenges. Saturn rules her 10th and 11th houses. The good aspect between her Libra Sun and Saturn in a Jupiter-ruled sign are an indication that she would receive rewards from her efforts. Saturn occupies a double-bodied sign and rules the 11th house of awards. Le Guin received two double book awards and was the first person to reach that milestone. A complete list of her literary awards would take several pages.

Le Guin's 2nd house Moon and Jupiter are the stars of the show. The Moon is conjunct Cursa (beta Eridanus, "the Footstool") and Jupiter is conjunct Rigel, Orion's foot in the whirlpool. Her creative output was inspired by current events and issues. Her books, in turn, had a massive ripple effect on readers, other writers, literary genres, publishing, radio, television, stage and cinema. Ursula's Moon is in the process of separating from a trine to Mercury and applying to conjunct Jupiter, making a translation of light between the planets. She took specifics from her own life, experiences, and environment (Mercury) and transformed them into grand adventures for the enjoyment of all (Jupiter).

An unusual feature of Le Guin's chart is stationary Pluto conjunct the IC. It's conjunct Castor, a writer's star. Her MC-IC axis is on the Gate of the Kosmocrator. Pluto has no visible major aspects. Unaspected planets are free agents that can do what they want to do without reference to other planets. There is, however, a hidden aspect from Mercury's antiscion at 20° Pisces. This secret trine gave depth, dimension and lyricism to her writing. She had profound empathy for her imaginary characters. Stories that don't evoke sympathy for the characters don't have legs. As she said, people need to see their experiences reflected in stories. Mercury's antiscion in Pisces speaks for misfits, people who don't feel like they belong, and people on a journey to find themselves through a range of awakening experiences and rites of passage. Ursula Le Guin's chart is both fateful and fortunate. Somebody had to tell these stories—Ursula embraced the mantle and wore it well.

Sample Draconic Charts

Secretariat

Secretariat was a champion thoroughbred horse that won the Triple Crown in 1973.[27] This is a helpful chart for astrologers who haven't worked with draconic charts before. Secretariat's natal North Node is at 11° Pisces. The Draconic Node at 0° Aries is only 19 degrees different; all of the planets and points in the natal chart shift 19 degrees to create the draconic chart.

This chart has extraordinary draconic connections. Draconic Neptune is conjunct his Ascendant, bringing oodles of glamour, public visibility and legendary status.

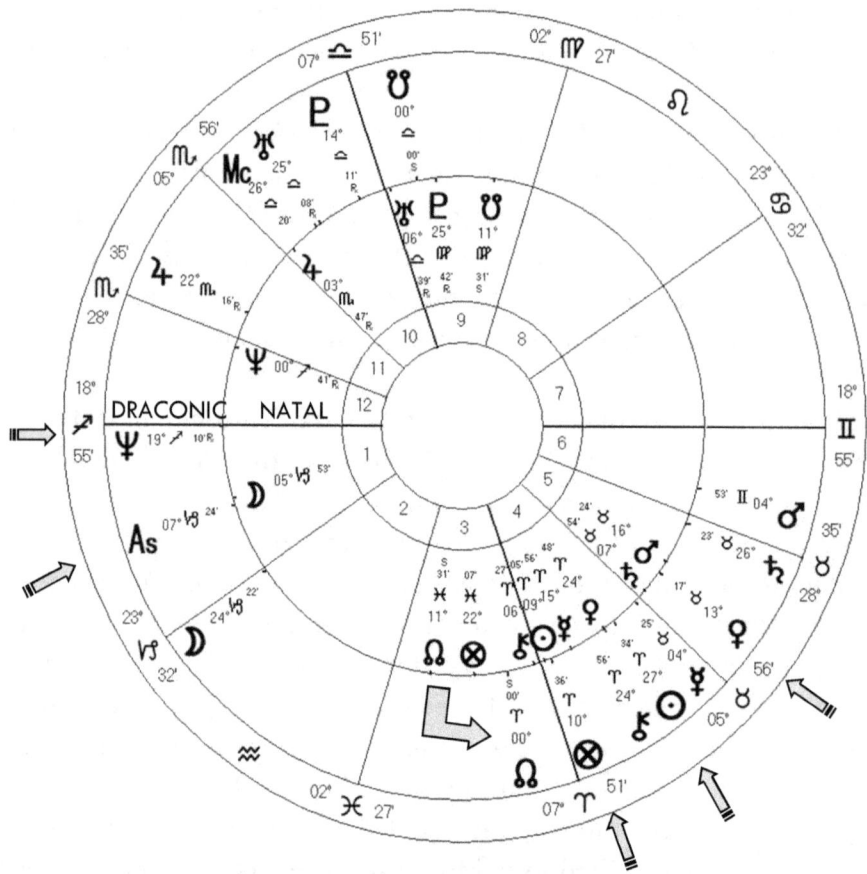

Secretariat—Natal and Draconic Charts
March 30, 1970, 12:10 am EST
Doswell, Virginia
Geocentric-Tropical
Inner wheel: Placidus-True Node Outer wheel: Draconic-True Node

The draconic Sun conjuncts natal Venus, which is already fired up in Aries. This Sun-Venus contact gives beauty and exceptionally strong will-power. It relates to the championship bloodlines of his sire Bold Ruler (4th house of the father and inheritances), his grandsire Nasrullah, and great grandsire Nearco.

This is more important than it might seem. Three horses are credited with establishing the thoroughbred breed in England during the 17th and 18th centuries: the Byerly Turk, the Darley Arabian, and the Godolphin Arabian. Byerly and Godolphin were progenitors of the first unbeatable racehorse—Eclipse—born in 1764 under a solar eclipse that passed over the British Islands as the foal was being born. A successful champion covers more mares and has far more offspring. There are very few significant champion bloodlines that all modern thoroughbreds can be traced to, and Eclipse is one of those progenitors.

Secretariat has become a great patriarch. Racehorses in the late 20th and early 21st centuries trace their lineage to Secretariat. Eight of twenty horses entered in the 2023 Kentucky Derby field were descendants. Since 2013, nineteen winners of 24 of the 29 Triple Crown races trace their lineage to Secretariat, and ten of them have Secretariat more than once in their pedigree. American Pharoah, a great-great-great grandson, won the Triple Crown in 2015. Justify, winner of the Triple Crown in 2018, is a sixth generation descendant of Secretariat through Storm Cat and AP Indy.[28]

Draconic Venus is conjunct natal Mars, giving Mars benefits from the sign ruler of Taurus. Venus-Mars combines beauty and strength, and the colors copper and red. It also shows a potent karmic connection to a woman—his owner, Penny Chenery Tweedy. There was a battle between family members over selling the horse to pay estate taxes at the beginning of 1973, but Penny was able to overcome her skeptical siblings and race Secretariat in the 1973 track season. Venus-Mars in the 5th house also indicates exceptional fertility. Secretariat sired 633 named foals over fifteen years as a stud. The Venus-Mars combination resonates with the Sun-Venus combination in the 4th house.

The draconic Ascendant is conjunct the natal Moon. This is similar to the concept of Chandra Lagna in Hindu astrology—using the Moon as the Ascendant. Secretariat's Moon is his rising planet. Although the Moon is in detriment in Capricorn, she enjoys a double mutual reception and trines with Mars and Saturn in Taurus. The Ascendant-Moon contact adds to Secretariat's public visibility and his sustained historic importance, both through his race career achievements, his still-standing track records, and as a genetic repository of a specific combination of American and European thoroughbred bloodlines. The draconic Part of Fortune is conjunct the exalted Sun in Aries. Secretariat was "most comfortable" being himself and fulfilling his incredible potential as an athlete. He seemed to know he was handsome and posed when cameras were around. He found everything he needed to be a champion within himself. The only thing jockey Ron Turcotte had to do was hang on for the ride. Secretariat was lucky to be himself, and he apparently reveled in it.

The second biwheel chart (*below*) has Secretariat's natal chart with the chart for the final Triple Crown race at Belmont Park on June 9, 1973. Secretariat not only won the race, but he won it by 31 lengths and set a world record by running the mile and a half race in 2:24 minutes.[29] None of his Triple Crown race times have been beaten yet. Franz notes that "Secretariat's record remains a benchmark of unparalleled excellence."[30]

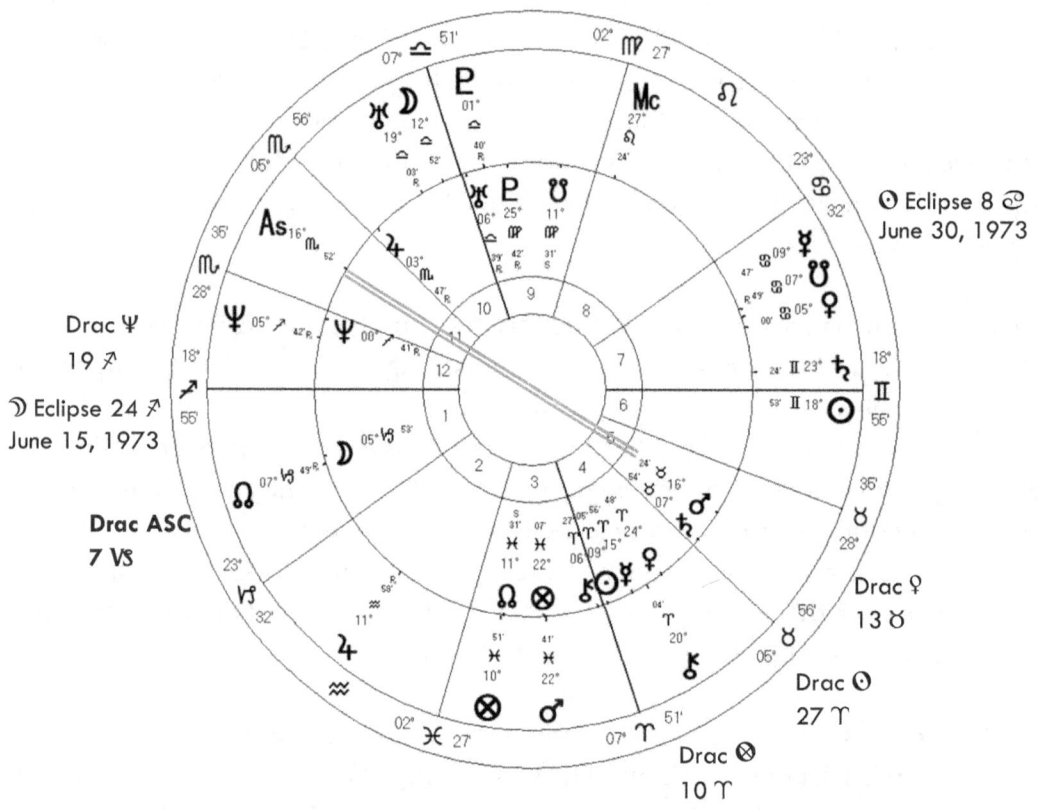

Secretariat Wins the Triple Crown
Inner Wheel—March 30, 1970, 12:10 am EST, Doswell, Virginia
Outer Wheel—June 9, 1973, 5:38 pm EDT, Long Island, New York
Geocentric-Tropical
Placidus-True Node

The draconic contacts are placed outside of the biwheel along with the eclipses that occurred in June 1973. The most notable combination in the transit chart is the triple conjunction of Venus, South Node, and Mercury in Cancer near the degree of the upcoming solar eclipse. This combination is in opposition to Secretariat's natal Moon, draconic Ascendant, and the transiting North Node. The transiting Nodal axis is tightly conjunct the draconic ASC-DSC axis. Secretariat enacted a collective fate by winning the race.

The powerful line-up on his draconic ASC-DSC axis indicates that his biological material (Cancer/Moon) was selectively chosen (Capricorn/Saturn) to win through hundreds of years of thoroughbred horse breeding programs. Cardinal signs are *speedy,* and Mercury-Venus-South Node in the face of Venus is the perfection of speed. Chapter 9 mentions that the South Node can be active during miraculous events. The transiting Sun in Gemini is conjunct his natal Descendent, activating draconic Neptune. Witnesses at Belmont as well as the millions of people who watched it on television were deeply moved by this race. It was described as a religious or mystical experience by hardened old track veterans.[31]

The transiting ASC at 16° Scorpio opposes Secretariat's natal Mars and draconic Venus conjunction. Everything was stacked in his favor for this race. Other owners scratched horses from the race because they knew Secretariat was just too good to beat. In a field of eight contenders, the only real challenger was Sham, a great horse, but not against Big Red. The two horses battled for the lead around the first turn and back stretch. By the second turn, Secretariat had taken the lead. Ron Turcotte had to turn around and look to see where the other horses were by the time they entered the final stretch.[32]

After winning a few more races in the 1973 racing season, Secretariat retired to the comfort of Claiborne Stables in Kentucky and started his career as a stud. That job didn't start smoothly, however. Secretariat's natal Sun-Uranus opposition shows that strange things were possible with this horse. There were concerns about his ability to sire offspring, so in early 1974, Secretariat covered a nurse mare named Leola. The mare was of Native American reservation Appaloosa descent. Secretariat's first son, born on November 15, 1974, was named First Secretary. The colt's buyer insisted on registering him as the son of Secretariat, and Claiborne Farm managers eventually relented.[33] Appaloosa owners are proud to report that their horses descend from the Secretariat line.

Alfred Hitchcock

Alfred Hitchcock is a famous mid-20th century film director known as the Master of Suspense.[34] Like Secretariat, the draconic Part of Fortune is conjunct his Sun. He fared best when he was being himself, and when he could freely utilize the entire scope of creativity offered by his Leo Sun.

The draconic South Node-natal Mars contact in Libra highlights his stylistic traits. His films advanced the genre of psychological thrillers using various techniques for keeping viewers off-balance and anxious. Libra confers cleverness and artistic nuances, and he used those skills to manipulate audience reactions. Hitchcock tapped into primal childhood fears about the monster under the bed or hiding the in closet. It's not what you *can see*, but what you *can't see* that

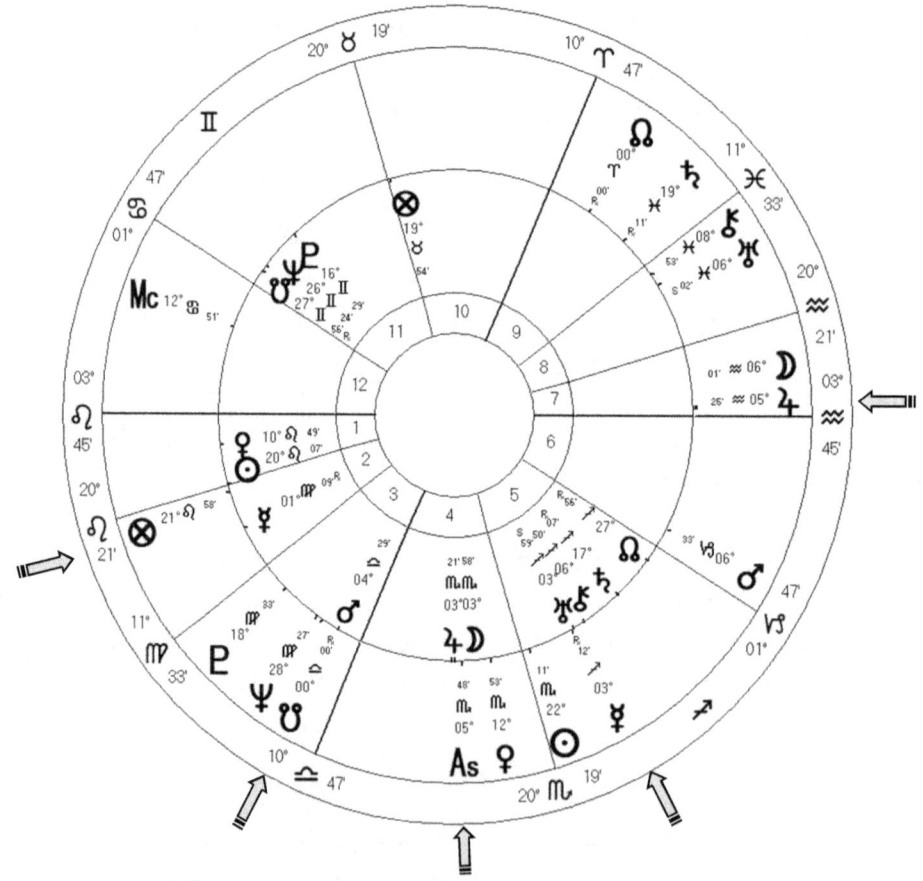

Alfred Hitchcock - Natal and Draconic Charts
August 13, 1899, 3:15 am UT
London, England
Geocentric-Tropical
Inner Wheel: Placidus-True Node.
Outer Wheel: Draconic-True Node

arouses anxieties. As he said, "There is no terror in the bang, only in the anticipation of it."[35] Rather than filming outright violence and gore, it's implied through suggestive camera angles and the performers' reactions. Mars is the father of Phobos (fears) and the South Node may stir up invisible sources of anxiety. Mars sextiles Venus in Leo, so this was expressed through the dramatic and artistic medium of cinema. He was able to possess (South Node) the audience through a 3rd house mode of communication.

Draconic Mercury and natal Uranus connect in Sagittarius and sextile South Node-natal Mars. Hitchcock's topical material was highly unusual. He tapped into the psychological ideas of his time, and those influenced his artistic choices and cinematic filming methods to maximize suspense. Hitchcock was also known for choosing icy blondes for lead roles. These women were muses for his fifth house creativity. Draconic Mercury indicates he selected a muse to fit each project. It was a necessity as actresses bolted after a film or two. Being the object of Hitchcock's obsessive attention was deeply uncomfortable, threatening and repellent. Uranus trines Hitchcock's Ascendant, and the Mercury-Uranus combo heightened his intellectual scope and scintillating originality.

The draconic Ascendant conjuncts his natal Jupiter-Moon conjunction in Scorpio, and draconic Jupiter-Moon conjunct the natal DSC. Public visibility is expanded as it is in Secretariat's chart. The dark mysterious side of Scorpio lends its influence. The rough outline of his profile and portly belly (Jupiter) was distinctive and became an iconic recognizable image. The silhouette was used in the introduction to the **Alfred Hitchcock Presents** television series. The Moon-Jupiter combinations also emphasize his creepy, obsessive voyeuristic traits that were so repellent to his muses.

Psycho, 1960

Hitchcock tapped Joseph Stefano to develop a script based on the 1959 book **Psycho** by Robert Bloch. Bloch's main character, Norman Bates, was an adaptation of serial killer Ed Gein. The violent twisted story made it difficult to raise funds for the film production. Paramount executives balked and refused to provide a production budget, so Hitchcock ended up financing the film himself in exchange for future earnings. He had to fight production code censors to keep certain scenes intact.

The film **Psycho** premiered at the DeMille Theater in New York City on June 16, 1960 and had its general release on September 8, 1960. It was Hitchcock's most

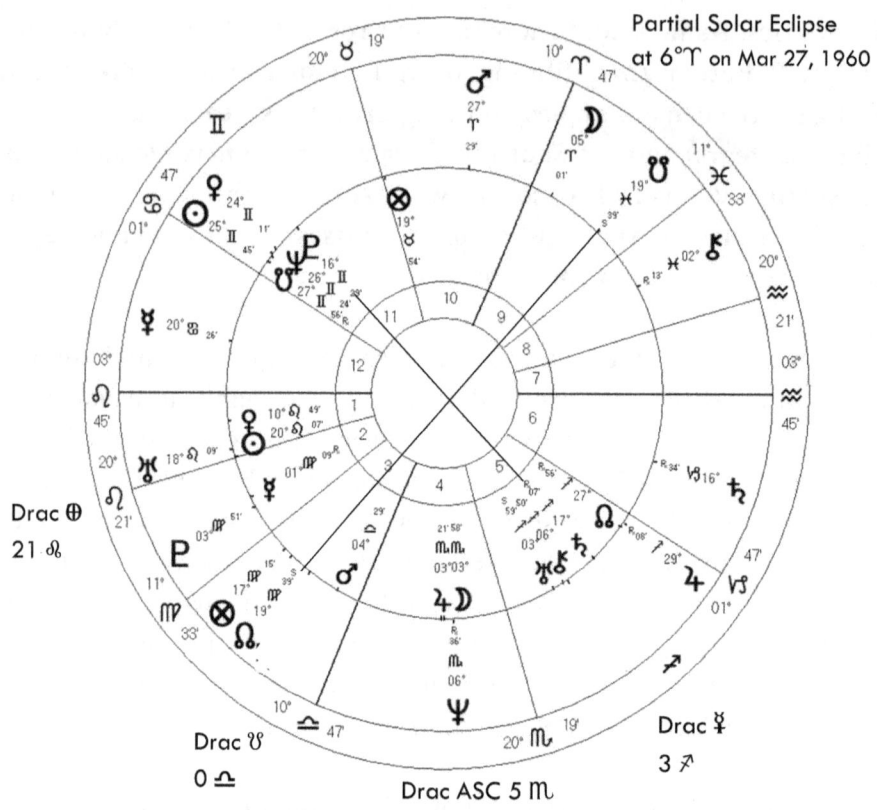

Alfred Hitchcock Premiere of *Psycho*
Inner Wheel: August 13, 1899, 3:15 am UT, London, England
Outer Wheel: June 16, 1960, 7:00 pm PDT, New York, NY
Geocentric-Tropical
Placidus-True Node

financially successful film and the highest-earning black and white film ever made. It is his most famous and influential film. It pushed the boundaries of cinematic violence, deviant behavior, and sexuality in American films. Transiting Uranus was conjunct his natal Sun–draconic PF contact, boosting his fame to new heights. A partial Solar Eclipse at 6° Aries in March 1960 and the transiting Moon activated his natal Mars-draconic South Node conjunction. While the film maximizes the fear factor, **Psycho** was like catnip to audiences, who lined up around the block to see it. The film is a strange blend of primal Mars-Aries fear factors wrapped in elegant Libran aesthetics.

Transiting Neptune is conjunct Hitchcock's natal Moon-Jupiter/draconic Ascendant. The release of this film cemented Hitchcock's reputation as cinema's Master of Suspense, and as one of the most gifted directors in film history. Neptune is associated with the cinema. The early-degree Scorpio line-up serves to accen-

Hitchcock and the Bates home set, 1960. by Hilton A Green. From Universal City image gallery at www.retroweb.com/universal-psycho.html. (Permission requested)

tuate the voyeuristic and psycho-analytical elements of the film. The initial murder is committed by a shadowy Scorpionic character. Scenes occur in contrasting light and darkness. Viewers witness Norman Bates' deterioration and final psychotic breakdown. Neptune is also linked to secrets. In the film's epilogue, Hitchcock instructs the audience not to reveal the plot twists or ending to people who haven't seen the film. The 4th house Scorpio cluster underscores the theme of family dysfunction. The element of Norman's interest in taxidermy and birds looming over characters in the scenes is an additional Scorpionic element. Transiting Neptune is conjunct Khambalia, a star in Virgo known to some as the Wizard's Star. **Psycho** was a project that allowed Hitchcock to utilize his entire bag of tricks—shadows and light, camera angles, suggestive dialogs, and concealed identities. Bernard Herrmann's dramatic film score heightened the psychological anguish and suspense experienced by viewers.

The American public's interest in serial killers had been piqued by the widely publicized, grisly murders of the Clutter family in Kansas a year earlier. This event inspired the book **In Cold Blood** by Truman Capote (published in 1965-66). Hitchcock dramatized the killer's inner psychological dynamics by leveraging his natal Moon-Jupiter in Scorpio—his instinctual urge to plumb the dark corners of human nature. Hitchock's Moon-Jupiter in Scorpio echo Truman Capote's Moon-Saturn conjunction in early Scorpio! The two men toyed with collective angst by becoming the dread-heads of the emerging true-crime/suspense/thriller genres during the 1960s. The draconic Ascendant-natal Moon-Jupiter contact impelled Hitchcock to make the depths and range of human nature visible (Moon-Jupiter) to others through his body (Ascendant) of films.

Summary

The focus in these delineations is limited to the draconic contacts. There are other natal placements activated by transits during Secretariat's Belmont victory and Hitchcock's landmark film. Both events represent career peaks that were witnessed by millions, and Neptune and the Moon are important in both charts. The natal-draconic connections activated by the transits suggest the fulfillment of specific fated or karmic potentials. The film **Psycho** (1960) and the 1973 Belmont Stakes race were both astonishing and unexpected but crucial to the collective zeitgeists of the 1960s and 1970s. Secretariat and Hitchcock both had the draconic Ascendant conjunct the Moon, and both were famous. The Moon symbolizes the public.

The selection of two natal-draconic chart samples that share Moon-Ascendant contacts was unintentional. They were selected as good examples of how draconic contacts emphasize particular traits and significant events. Two charts don't provide enough evidence to make any definitive statements, but they do suggest that draconic contacts to the natal Ascendant and contacts by the draconic Ascendant are highly significant and potentially fateful. The sample charts feature four or five draconic contacts. This is a normal amount. As these two charts show, draconic contacts to natal placements show what makes individuals distinctive and memorable, and highlights the traits and characteristics that make the greatest impression on others. They also show the most likely influences that are portals for a person's fate, fortune, providence, and destiny to manifest. These can be interpreted through planets, stars, signs and houses.

The Milky Way by EH

Conclusion

This book represents a quest to gain greater insights on ancient soul travel theories set forth in **Hamlet's Mill**, and to share how these ideas can be applied by astrologers. Sources ranged from primary resource materials from ancient cultures to mythologies, books about ancient religions and philosophies, and translations of ancient astrology books. College lecture notes by the late Professor Tolkien now published in book form by his son Christopher include scholarly writing on topics outside of his Middle Earth series and transcriptions of his lecture notes. Those are additional sources of insights.

It's difficult to provide a complete list of reference materials because of their sheer quantity and diversity. **Hamlet's Mill** has a detailed although rather dated bibliography. The evidence of extremely early, possibly pre-historic, human awareness of the Cosmic Axis presented in **Hamlet's Mill** has grown since the book's publication in 1969. Interest in classical astrology, improved translations of Egyptian funerary scrolls and art, and the new field of archeo-astrology have contributed much ponderous material documenting an enduring curiosity about metempsychosis (soul migration).

New Age books by contemporary psychics and channelers sometimes present far-flung notions about reincarnation. Reading those kinds of books in the 1980s and 1990s made me increasingly skeptical. Paths taken by souls to and from the afterlife aren't mentioned, yet it's clear that this is a crucial element of ancient thinking on the subject. Delving into the earliest theories revealed that the how's and why's of early soul migration theories were invariably entwined with lore about the Cosmic Axis. Each is intrinsic to the other. The central goal of the mystery cults was to prepare initiates for an unhindered journey into the afterlife. Members were encouraged to live a "good and blameless life" to minimize afterlife penalties and keep their souls as clean as possible. They memorized passphrases to use at gates or portals along the cosmic pathways.

In light of the overwhelmingly pervasive ancient beliefs in soul travel, it's sad that the major religions of the Age of Pisces omit information about reincarnation and went to great lengths to purposely exclude and suppress it. The harsh and sometimes violent means that were used to eradicate this knowledge merit reflection on what the arbiters hoped to gain through such censorship. Concepts of the afterlife changed radically after the 4th century CE. Mystery cult practices persisted in secret for centuries but eventually their beliefs and lore retreated into the shadows of Western culture.

The reader must decide if reincarnation is a valid concept and if any of the ideas presented in this book are worth embracing. Another question for consideration is whether the individual should exert a conscious effort during life to enhance the soul's journey after death.

Astrologers may consider whether birth charts offer a map—not just for the current life—but also of the soul's purpose, of the paths the soul has taken into the current incarnation, and if the cosmic soul portals described herein are worthy of attention.

A quote from the inimitable satirist Terry Pratchett seems appropriate for the end of this book. "No one is finally dead until the ripples they cause in the world die away, until the clock wound up winds down, until the wine she made has finished its ferment, until the crop they planted is harvested. The span of someone's life is only the core of their actual existence."[1]

But my favorite quote is: "It would be a very dull world if we were all the same."[2]

References

A Brief Introduction
Pg i, 1 Georgio de Santillana and Hertha von Dechend, **Hamlet's Mill**. Nonpariel Books, 1969.

Part I: The Cosmos and Soul Travel
Chapter 1. Time and Ancient Wisdom............pg 1
Pg i, 1 Aristotle, **Nichomachean Ethics**. H. Rackham, translator. Loeb Classical Library, 1934.

Chapter 2. The Egyptian Cosmos............pg 7
Pg 9, 1 Joanne Conman, **Egyptian Sky Lore: Rethinking the Conventional Wisdom**. Disinformation Books, 2014.
Pg 9, 2 Demetra George, Star Decans lecture, November 20, 2021. Astrology Univ.
Pg 10, 3 Robert Bauval and Thomas Brophy PhD. **Imhotep the African: Architect of the Cosmos**. Disinformation Books, 2014
Pg 12, 4 James P. Allen, **The Ancient Pyramid Texts**. Society of Biblical Literature, 2005. https://archive.org/details/the-ancient-egyptian-pyramid-texts_202103/mode/2up

Chapter 3. The Mesopotamian Cosmos............pg 13
Pg 17, 1 Gavin White, **Babylonian Star-Lore, An Illustrated Guide to the Star-lore and Constellations of Ancient Babylonia**. Solaria Publications, 2007.
Pg 17, 2 James Herschel Holden, translator. **Rhetorius the Egyptian**. AFA, Inc. 2009.
Pg 17, 3 Claudius Ptolemy, **Tetrabiblos**. Many editions available.
Pg 18, 4 Titus Burchardt. **Mystical Astrology According to Ibn 'Arabi**. Fons Vitae, 2001.

Chapter 4. Changes in Cosmic Time............pg 20
Pg 22, 1 Robert Hand, **Essays in Astrology**. "The Age and Constellation of Pisces". Zip Dobyns gives more information in the article "Astrological Ages" with information from Robert Hand and Mark Pottenger). Los Angeles Community Church of Religious Science, Inc., 1984. See: http://ccrsdodona.org/m_dilemma/1984/gem/ages.html
Pg 23, 2 Nicholas Campion, **The Book of World Horoscopes**. Wessex Astrologer, 2004, p 485.
Pg 24, 3 Carl Jung. **Aion**. Princeton University Press, 1979.
Pg 24, 4 Neil Gaiman. **American Gods**. Harper Torch, 2001
Pg 24, 5 Vivian Robson, **Fixed Stars and Constellations**. pp 184-85
Pg 28, 6 Nicholas Mann. **Avebury Cosmos**. O Books, 2015, p 5.
Pg 31, 7, Mann, ibid, pp 244-247.
Pg 33, 8 White, **Babylonian Star-Lore**, 2007, ibid.

Chapter 5. Metaphysical Mythology...pg 37

Pg 38, 1 J. R. R. Tolkien. **The Silmarillion**. edited by Christopher Tolkien and Guy Gavriel Kay. Allen and Unwin, 1977 (published posthumously).

Pg 40, 2 Marcus Minucius Felix, **Octavius: A Dialogue**. Translated by Sir David Dalrymple, Murray & Cochran for T. Cadell, 1781; reprinted by Gale Ecco, Print Editions, 2018.

Pg 41, 3 Marija Gimbutas, **The Living Goddesses**. University of California Press, 1999 (published posthumously).

See also: Marija Gimbutas. **The Goddesses and Gods of Old Europe: Myths and Cult Images**. New and updated edition, University of California Press, 1982.

Pg 42, 4 Jean Auel, Earth's Children (**Clan of the Cave Bear**) series. Random House Publishing Group, 1980-2011.

Pg 42, 5 From the **Mahabarata**. See: Wendy O'Flaherty. **Hindu Myths**. Penguin Books, 1975.

Pg 44, 6 **The Poetic Edda** (also called The Elder Edda). Translated by Henry Adams Bellows, Dover Publications, 2007. See the *Hymiskviða*

Pg 44, 7 Saxo Grammaticus, **The Gesta Danorum** (13th c CE). Published as **The Nine Books of the Danish History of Saxo Grammaticus**. Translated by Oliver Elton. Norroena Society, 1905. Available at The Gutenberg Project, see: https://www.gutenberg.org/files/1150/1150-h/1150-h.htm#link2H_4_0001

Pg 44, 8 Snorri, Stuluson, **The Prose Edda** (or Edda Saemundar). Translator Jesse L Byock. Penguin Classics, 2006. Story in *Skaldskaparmal*.

Pg 46, 9 Vivian Robson, **The Fixed Stars and Constellations in Astrology**. Cecil Palmer, 1923, original edition (many reprints available), pg 43.

Pg 46, 10 The Codex Regius or "King's Book" (circa 1270) is an Icelandic codex in which poems from the Poetic Edda are preserved. The third poem in the Codex is "The Vafþrúðnismál" (Vafþrúðnir's sayings). Odin and the jötunn Vafþrúðnir engage in a battle of wits exchanging details about Norse cosmogony, stanzas 6 – 55. See **The Poetic Edda**, Bellows, Dover, 2007 (ibid).

Pg 48, 11 **The Odyssey of Homer**. Translated by Richard Lattimore. Harper Perennial, 1965.

Pg 48, 12 Virgil (Publius Vergilius Maro), **The Aeneid**. (19 BCE), translated by John Dryden at http://classics.mit.edu/Virgil/aeneid.html

Pg 49, 13 **The Epic of Gilgamesh**, translated by N. K. Sandars. Penguin Classics, 1960.

Pg 49, 14 Plato, **The Symposium**. Christopher Gill, editor and translator. Penguin Classics, 1952.

Pg 49, 15 Ovid. **The Metamorphosis**. Translated by Mary Innes. Penguin Books, 1955.

Pg 49, 16 Pseudo-Apollodorus, **Bibliotheca** (The Library). Written 1st – 2nd c CE. English translation by Sir James G. Frazer, Harvard University Press, 1921. Loeb Classical Library edition (reprint) at The Internet Archive, see: https://archive.org/details/apollodorus-library-loeb-frazer

Pg 50, 17, Robson, ibid, pp 46-47.

Pg 50, 18 Aesop, **The Complete Fables**. Penguin Classics, 1998.

Pg 50, 19 Robert Graves. **The Greek Myths, Complete Edition.** Penguin Books, 1955.
Pg 51, 20 Jesse L. Byock, translator, The Saga of the Volsungs. Penguin Classics, 2000.
P 51, 21 A. T. Hatto, translator, **The Nibelungenlied: Prose Translation.** Penguin Classics, 1965.
P 51, 22 Lady Charlotte Guest, translator, **The Mabinogion.** Bernard Quaritch, 1877. The Tale of Taliesin, pp. 471 - 494, at Sacred Texts, see: https://sacred-texts.com/neu/celt/mab/mab32.htm

Chapter 6. The Greek Cosmos..pg 53

Pg 54, 1 Homeric Hymn 2 to Demeter, line 347. **Hesiod, Homeric Hymns, Epic Cycle, Homerica.** Translated by Hugh G. E. White, Loeb Classical Library, Harvard University Press, 1914.

Pg 55, 2 Orphic Hymn #69. **The Orphic Hymns.** Translated by Apostolos Athanassakis, Scholars Press, 1977.

Pg 55, 3 **Sophocles I: Oedipus the King, Oedipus at Colonus, and Antigone, The Complete Greek Tragedies** edited by David Grene and Richard Lattimore. Pocket Books, 1972.

Pg 55, 4 Euripides, **Orestes and Other Plays.** Philip Vellacott, translator. Penguin Classics, 1972.

Pg 55, 5 Theogony in **Hesiod, Homeric Hymns, Epic Cycle, Homerica.** Translated by Hugh G. E. White, Loeb Classical Library, Harvard University Press, 1914.

Pg 58, 6 Hesiod, **Works and Days.** (in **Homerica**), 1914, ibid.

Pg 59, 7 **Plato's Timaeus.** Translated by Peter Kakavage. Focus Publications, 2001.

Pg 59, 8 Plato, **Republic, Volume II: Books 6 - 10.** Christopher Emly-Jones and William Preddy, translators. Loeb Classical Library, 2013. Book X: The Story of Er.

Pg 59, 9 Plato, **Phaedrus.** Christopher Rowe, translator. Penguin Classics, 2005.

Pg 61, 10 Virgil, **The Aeneid**, ibid.

Pg 61, 11 Virgil, **The Aeneid**, Book VI "The Kingdom of the Dead", lines 836-869. The final lines of the section:

> a few of us even hold these fields of joy
> till the long days, a cycle of time seen through,
> cleanse our hard, inveterate stains and leave us clear
> ethereal sense, the eternal breath of fire purged and pure.
> But all the rest, once they have turned the wheel of time
> for a thousand years: God calls them forth to the Lethe,
> great armies of souls, their memories blank so that
> they may revisit the overarching world once more
> and begin to long to return to bodies yet again."
> (translated by Robert Fagles, © 2006)

Pg 62, 12 **The Bhagavad Gita As It Is.** Translated and annotated by A. C. Bhaktivedanta Swami Pradhupada. Bhaktivedanta Book Trust 1968.

Pg 62, 13 Heraklitus, **Fragments**. Brooks Haxton, translator. Penguin Classics, English and Greek Edition, 2003. Quote from Fragr 60. Heraklitus continues in Frag. 62: "Mortal immortals, immortal mortals: the former ones living the latter's death, the latter ones dying the formers' life." That is – the gods live through humans, and they become aware of their own immortality through the contrast of human or earthly mortality.

Pg 63, 14 Plotinus (3rd c CE), **The Enneads: The Six Enneads, Complete—The Philosophy of Neo-Platonism.** James MacKenna, et al, translators. Pantianos Classics, 1917. Book VI: Hypostasis of the Soul.

Pg 63, 15 "In Adam were contained..." quotes in **Hamlet's Mill**, Part 11, Chapter 22 "The Adventure and the Quest", reference: A. Eisenmenger, **Entdecktes Judenthzcm** (1711), vol. 2, p. 16 (Emek hamelech).

Pg 63, 16 Noel Langley and Hugh Lynn Cayce, **Edgar Cayce on Reincarnation**. Paperback Library, 1967.

Pg 63, 17 **The Bhagavad Gita As It Is.** Bhaktivedanta Book Trust, 1968, ibid.

Pg 63, 18 Rollo May, **Freedom and Destiny**. Norton, 1981.

Pg 68, 19 **The Bible**, Psalm 42:7

Pg 68, 20 **Wanted**. Universal Pictures, 2008.

Pg 69, 21 Nigel Pennick, **Pagan Magic of the Northern Tradition: Customs, Rites and Ceremonies**. Destiny Books, 2015.

Chapter 7. Mystery Cults and Soul Travel..............................pg 73

Pg 73, 1 Cicero, **De re Publica (On the Republic), De Legibus (On the Laws)**. Clinton W. Keyes, translator. Loeb Classical Library No. 213, 1928. II.14.

Pg 73, 2 Joscelyn Godwin. **Mystery Religions in the Ancient World**. Harper and Row, 1981.

Pg 73, 3 **The Chronographia of Michael Psellos**. E. R. A. Sewter, translator. Routledge & Kegan Paul, 1953. See The Internet Archive at: https://archive.org/details/michael-psellus-chronographia

Pg 74, 4 G. R. S. Mead, **Orpheus**, 1896. Barns & Noble, Inc., 1965. Chapter 4, General Outline of Orphic Theogony.

Pg 74, 5 Albert Lebegue and Georg Kaibel, **Inscriptiones graecae Siciliae et Italiae**. Berolini, 1890, number 641.

Pg 74, 6 **The Orphic Hymns**. Athanassakis translation, ibid.

Pg 75, 7, **The Orphic Hymns**, Athanassakis translation, ibid.

Pg 75, 8 Amos Bronsen Alcott, **Orphic Sayings.** *The Dial*, 1840-1842. See: http://www.alcott.net/cgi-bin/archive/alcott/Orphic_Sayings.html

Pg 76, 9 Brian P. Copenhaver, editor. **Hermetica: The Greek Corpus Hermeticum and the Latin Asclepius in a New English Translation, with Notes and Introduction.** Cambridge University Press, 1995.

See also: Clement Salaman, Dorine van Oyen, William Wharton, et al. **The Way of Hermes: New Translations of the Corpus Hermeticum and The Definitions of Hermes Trismegistus to Asclepius**. Inner Traditions, 2004.

Pg 78, 10 Virgil, **Aeneid** (ibid), vi 740-746.

Pg 78, 11 **Plutarch's Moralia in Sixteen Volumes, XV Fragments.** F. H. Sandbach, translator. Loeb Classical Library, 1969/1987. **Fragment 178**, pp 317-318. See: https://archive.org/details/moraliainfiftee15plut/page/316/mode/2up

Pg 78, 12 Margherita Guarducci, **Epigrafia Greca**, Vol IV. Epigrafi Sacre Pagane e Cristiane. Istituto Poligrafico Dello Stato, 1978, p 263. https://archive.org/details/margherita-guarducci-epigrafia-greca

Part II: Applied Astrology—Planets, Stars and Souls
Chapter 8. Soul Portals..pg 83

Pg 83, 1 **Heraclides of Pontus: Texts and Translations.** Editor Eckart Schutrumpf. Transaction Publishers, 2008.

Pg 83, 2 Porphyry, **On the Cave of the Nymphs in the Thirteenth Book of the Odyssey.** Translation by Thomas Taylor and John M Watkins, 1917. Section 11. https://www.tertullian.org/fathers/porphyry_cave_of_nymphs_02_translation.htm

See also: Macrobius, **Commentary on the Dream of Scipio.** Translation by William Harris Stahl, Columbia University Press, 1990.

Pg 93, 3 Terry Pratchett, **Witches Abroad.** Harper Torch, 1991.

Pg 94, 4 Bernadette Brady. **Brady's Book of Fixed Stars.** Samuel Weiser, 1998.

Pg 94, 5 Reinhold Ebertin and Georg Hoffman, **Fixed Stars and Their Interpretation.** AFA, 2009 (1976). (the star positions are out of date)

Pg 94, 6 Vivian Robson, **The Fixed Stars and Constellations in Astrology.** Cecil Palmer, 1923, original edition. Many reprints available. (the star positions are badly out of date)

Pg 94, 7 Elizabeth Hazel, **Little Book of Fixed Stars**, second edition. Kozmic Kitchen Press, 2020.

Pg 94, 8 Diana K. Rosenberg, **Secrets of the Ancient Skies, Volumes 1 & 2.** Ancient Skies Press, 2012.

Pg 94, 9 Richard Hinckley Allen, **Star Names: Their Lore and Meaning.** G. E. Stechert, 1899, original edition. Dover Books, 1963. A free pdf of the original edition is available at the Internet Archive: https://archive.org/details/allen-r.-star-names

Chapter 9. The Moon's Nodes and Mercury............................pg 97

Pg 102, 1 Andrew Foss, **Yoga of the Planets: Their Mantras and Philosophy.** CreateSpace, 2016.

Pg 103, 2 Gary Caton, **Mercury Tripticha.** Rubedo Press, 2017.

Pg 104, 3 Conman, **Egyptian Sky Lore**, ibid.

Pg 105, 4 Ram Shankar Misra, **The Integral Advaitism of Sri Aurobindo.** Motilal Banarsidass, 1998.

Pg 105, 5 Fritjof Capra, **The Tao of Physics.** Bantam, 1975.

Pg 106, 6 Richard Hooker, **M*A*S*H*.** William Morrow, 1968.

Pg 111, 7 Liz Greene, **The Astrology of Fate**. Weiser Books, 1984.

Pg 111, 8 Howard Sasportas, **The Gods of Change: Pain, Crisis, and the Transits of Uranus, Neptune, and Pluto**. The Penguin Group, 1989.

Chapter 10. Draconic Charts and Other Portals..................pg 113

Pg 116, 1 Elizabeth Hazel, **Antiscia: Secrets in the Mirror**. Kozmic Kitchen Press, 2020.

Pg 116, 2 Robert Zoller, **The Arabic Parts in Astrology: A Lost Key to Prediction**. Inner Traditions, 1989.

Pg 116, 3 Chris Brennan, "The Theoretical Rationale Underlying the Seven Hermetic Lots." Self-published paper available as a free pdf at https://www.chrisbrennanastrologer.com

Pg 116, 4 (*in footnote*) Julius Firmicus Maternus, **Mathesis**. Translated and annotated by James Herschel Holden. AFA, 2010.

Chapter 11: Applied Astrology: Sample Charts
Syd Barrett..pg 121

Pg 121, 1 General biographical information: https://en.wikipedia.org/wiki/Syd_Barrett

Pg 124, 2 Pink Floyd, **Piper at the Gates of Dawn** (LP). EMI Columbia, August 4, 1967.

Pg 124, 3 Kenneth Grahame, **The Wind in the Willows**. Methuen and Co., 1908 (original edition).

Pg 124, 4 and 5 Padraig O'Connor, "Song of the Week Blog: Wined & Dined – Syd Barrett." July 29, 2013. Quotes Malcolm Dome and Robyn Hitchcock, doesn't provide sources, sources not found. At: https://songoftheweekblog.wordpress.com/2013/07/29/song-of-the-week-48-wined-dined-syd-barrett/

Pg 125, 6 Padraig O'Connor, ibid.

Pg 125, 7 and 8 – Nick Kent, "The Cracked Ballad of Syd Barrett." *New Musical Express*, April 13, 1974. Article posted at: https://sydbarrett.net/syd-barrett-articles/the-cracked-ballad-of-syd-barrett/

Dane Rudhyar..pg 128

Pg 128, 9 Candy Hillenbrand, "The Legacy of Dane Rudhyar (1895 – 1985)". *The Mountain Astrologer*, Dec 2014-Jan 2015 issue, pp 40-45.

Pg 130, 10 Hillenbrand, ibid, pg 43.

Audie Murphy: Two Charts Make Twice the Man ....pg 131

Pg 131, 11 General biographical information: https://en.wikipedia.org/wiki/Audie_Murphy

Pg 131, 12 Astro-Databank (ADB) notes Gary Noel's 2024 discovery of Murphy's birth certificate. An image of the birth certificate is included on the page. https://www.astro.com/astro-databank/Murphy,_Audie

Pg 135, 13 Philip Martin, "Critical Mass: Unassuming Audie Murphy a true American hero." Arkansas Online, July 19, 2020. https://www.arkansasonline.com/news/2020/jul/19/unassuming-audie-murphy-a-true-american-hero/

Pg 138, 14 Philip Martin, ibid.

Pg 138, 15 Philip Martin, ibid.

Pg 139, 16 Walter Cronkite announces Murphy's death on the CBS Evening News, May 31, 1971. Video at: https://www.youtube.com/watch?v=svyABpepdck

Amalie "Emmy" Noether..pg140

Pg 140, 17 General biographical data: https://en.wikipedia.org/wiki/Emmy_Noether
    See also: History Working Group, "Emmy Noether's Paradise." Institute for Advanced Study, 2017. https://www.ias.edu/ideas/2017/emmy-noether's-paradise

Pg 140, 18 Leon M. Lederman and Christopher T. Hill, **Symmetry and the Beautiful Universe**. Prometheus Books, 2004, pg 73.

Pg 142, 19 Albert Einstein, "The Late Emmy Noether: Professor Einstein Writes in Appreciation of a Fellow-Mathematician". Letter to the *New York Times*, May 4, 1935.

Pg 142, 20 Auguste Dick, **Emmy Noether: 1882-1935**. Birkhauser, 1981, pg 100.

Pg 143, 21 B. L. van der Waerden, "Nachruf auf Emmy Noether." (Obituary of Emmy Noether), *Mathematische Annalen*, Number 111:469-474.

Ursula Le Guin..pg 145

Pg 145, 22 General biographical information: https://www.ursulakleguin.com/biography and https://en.wikipedia.org/wiki/Ursula_K._Le_Guin

Pg 147, 23 David Streitfeld, "Ursula Le Guin Has Earned a Rare Honor. Just Don't Call Her a Science Fiction Writer." *New York Times*, August 28, 2016. https://www.nytimes.com/2016/08/29/books/ursula-le-guin-has-earned-a-rare-honor-just-dont-call-her-a-sci-fi-writer.html

Pg 147, 24 Margaret Atwood, "We lost Ursula Le Guin when we needed her most" *Washington Post*, March 7, 2019.

pg 147, 25 Maria Popova, "Ursula Le Guin on Art, Storytelling, and the Power of Language to Transform and Redeem." The Marginalian, Jan 30, 2018. at www.themarginalian.org

pg 148, 26 Victoria Brownworth, "Ursula K. Le Guin: A Tribute." *The Lambda Literary Review* Jan 5, 2018 at www.lambdaliterary.org/2018/01/ursula-le-guin/

Sample Draconic Charts

Secretariat..pg 150

Pg 150, 27 General biographical information from: Bill Nack, **Secretariat: The Making of a Champion**. Arthur Fields Books, 1975 (original edition). This book is the source of Secretariat's birth data, p 25.
    See also: Kate Chenery Tweedy and Leeanne Meadows Ladin, **Secretariat's Meadow**. Dementi Milestone Publishing, 2010.

Pg 151, 28 Patricia McQueen, "Not just an iconic racehorse: Secretariat's impact on the Triple Crown as a sire." *Thoroughbred Racing Commentary*, June 6, 2023. https://www.thoroughbredracing.com/articles/5916/not-just-legennot-just-iconic-racehorse-secretariats-impact-triple-crown-siredary-racehorse-tracing-secretariats-impact-triple-crown-sire/

Pg 152, 29 Oliver Franz, "Triple Crown Legacy: Secretariat's Statistical Dominance in the 1973 Belmont Stakes." Minitab Statistical Software blog, May 23, 2024. https://blog.minitab.com/en/triple-crown-legacy-secretariats-statistical-dominance-in-the-1973-belmont-stakes

Pg 152, 30 Franz, ibid.

Pg 153, 31 Nack, ibid.

Pg 153, 32 The video of the 1973 Belmont Stakes race is well worth watching. The most complete videos from the CBS broadcast have been posted by Vintage North American Horse Racing. Part 4 (10:55 min) features pre-race commentary as the contenders are being loaded into the gate and the great Chic Anderson's classic call of the race. At 5:51 minutes, Anderson says "Secretariat is widening now. He is moving like a tremendous machine!" The phrase "tremendous machine" is a perfect description for an athlete with a Capricorn Moon trine Mars and Saturn in Taurus. Anderson stated that Secretariat was 25 lengths in front, but 31 lengths is the correct amount. https://www.youtube.com/watch?v=kZ6Xu0SFqH0&list=PL8DB7B40B0CF4DD03&index=15

Pg 153, 33 The birth of First Secretary was reported in an editorial in **Blood-Horse** magazine, January 1974. There are doubts about a US breeder's certificate for the foal. The Canadian Appaloosa registry collaborated with the American Appaloosa registry, and it seems that owner Jack Nankivil got the foal registered without a US breeder's certificate. First Secretary's November birth date made him ineligible to race, so he worked as a stud and sired 247 foals. Information from a Facebook post "The Story of First Secretary" on the "We Love Secretariat" page, August 30, 2024.

Alfred Hitchcock..**pg154**

Pg 154, 34 General biographical information: https://en.wikipedia.org/wiki/Alfred_Hitchcock

Pg 155, 35 The quote is attributed to Alfred Hitchcock in Leslie Halliwell, **Halliwell's Filmgoer's Companion 1984**. HarperCollins, 1984.

Conclusion..**pg 161**

Pg 162, 1 Terry Pratchett, **Reaper Man: A Discworld® Novel**. Harper, 1991.

Pg 162, 2 Terry Pratchett, **Unseen Academicals**. Doubleday/Transworld Publishers Ltd., 2009, pg 78 (paperback edition).

About the Author

Elizabeth Hazel is a professional astrologer, tarotist and rune-reader, an author and lecturer. She is a long-time board member and president of the SMARRT/Ann Arbor chapter of NCGR.

Elizabeth has occupied various roles in the NCGR Publications group and is a frequent contributor to a wide range of publications. She presents webinars for astrology groups around the country and has spoken at UAC, GLAC, SOTA, ConVocation, and other astrology and tarot conferences. She does private consultations and chart interpretations, including fixed star and antiscia analysis.

Her works include **Tarot Decoded** (Weiser, 2004) and **The Whispering Tarot** deck and book (Kozmic Kitchen Press, 2008, available from the author). Other works include **Little Book of Fixed Stars, Antiscia: Secrets in the Mirror**, and **Twelve-House Tarot Spreads** from Kozmic Kitchen Press.

Elizabeth lives in Northwest Ohio with Mister Gustav, an extra-large ginger kitty who was rescued from the jaws of death in 2022 and now lives a life of opulent luxury.

Contact: ehazel1731@gmail.com.

Mister Gustav
Bamboozler-in-Chief

More by Elizabeth Hazel

Books are available through Amazon.
The Whispering Tarot deck and book are
Available directly from the author.

www.ingramcontent.com/pod-product-compliance
Lightning Source LLC
Chambersburg PA
CBHW060233240426
43671CB00016B/2930